ONE MAN'S DREAM

The Spirit of the Rubel Castle

D1605164

By

David C. Traversi

ISBN O-9744532-0-X

ONE MAN'S DREAM

The Spirit of the Rubel Castle

TABLE OF CONTENTS

AUTHOR'S PREFACE

The opportunity to explore one of the more unique phenomenons of our time was irresistible. A good friend, Bill Graham, introduced me to Michael Rubel and his Castle several years ago, providing entrance into a world that seemed beyond the parameters of normal adult experience. It is the world of imagination, a locale most of us leave behind in the process of maturing and becoming responsible. Undoubtedly, the power of imagination is one of the greatest sources of freedom, but too often it is submerged in the perceived demands of daily life. We are thereby deprived of one of the richest resources available for living a full and rewarding life.

It was at once apparent that Michael Rubel had not only retained his imagination throughout adulthood, but had actually created a life for himself and those around him that had a fairy-tale quality of surrealism. Something in Michael and the influence he had on the lives of his friends re-awakened the imagination which had been buried by years of dealing with the realities of life as a lawyer, and demanded that I participate, if only vicariously, in the spirit of the Castle builders at Glendora. It has been a journey I will cherish forever, leaving me trusting in the same power that Michael knows is there to provide for all of our needs. It is my privilege to tell you the story of Rubelia.

David C. Traversi

ACKNOWLEDGEMENTS

This work would have been impossible without the help and support of many people who gave unstintingly of their time and talents to assist the author. There are far too many to mention individually, but a few must be singled out for particular recognition since their efforts were both unique and vital to any attempt to relate the story in a meaningful manner.

Initially, MICHAEL for the hours spent sharing himself, his home and his life with the author, making it such an enjoyable and satisfying endeavor. For his patience in helping to put together a tale which covers most of his life, and his perspective which was invaluable for organizing it into a meaningful, flowing account of a most unusual existence. There are many anecdotes and stories of incidents which are so unique, that many of his friends will tell you that the stories change with each re-telling. In fact, Kaia says that Michael's biggest problem is not remembering things that didn't happen. But Michael's answer to this is couched in one of Grandfather Deuel's maxims, "Don't bore people with the truth – just show them the baby." And the baby, in this case, the Castle, is standing there for all to see and forever verify that Michael has the power to make his dreams materialize.

KAIA POORBAUGH, Michael's wife, who was really the historian for the Castle and recorded progress over the years with photo albums which eventually amounted to 42 in number. For her help in selecting the albums that would contain the most helpful pictures for the purposes of this work, saving countless hours of time during the research process. For her part in making the Castle such an enjoyable home for the author during his stays and especially for providing her perspective on the events chronicled here during the ferry trips to and from the airport.

JOE and IDA FRICASSE, the owners and publishers of the *Glendoran* magazine for their generosity and graciousness in allowing unrestricted access to their published materials about Michael and the Castle over a period of many years. This wonderful publication is rich with the fabric of a community that has retained its identity despite the inevitable growth, and Joe and Ida are in large part responsible for preserving this identity. The author is deeply indebted and without them this work would not have been possible

WARREN BOWEN and DARWIN HANNIBAL. They are part of an informal social club with Michael dating back to 1935, called the "Romeos." It is an acronym for "Real Old Men Eating Out," or "Real Odd Men Eating Out," depending on whom you listen to. Warren and Darwin provided invaluable assistance by taking a great number of digital pictures of the Castle, its grounds, old photos and Michael, and reduced them to compact discs for usage in the book. And especially to the Romeos for so graciously including the author at their luncheon meetings.

DICK MACY, another of the Romeos and a most active Castle docent, for the information acquired while accompanying him during one of his guided tours through the Castle and its grounds, providing still another perspective of this unique phenomenon. He also authored a pamphlet entitled *Rubelia Castle* that included information and an organizational scheme which made the Rubel story easier to frame into a workable context.

BILL GRAHAM, for the original introduction to Michael and for much of the history of this amazing project, and especially for insight into the spirit which bound the Pharm volunteers together and brought the Castle to fruition.

GRANDFATHER HARRY A. DEUEL, deceased, for the wisdom and humor which he infused into this saga, and especially for his maxims which appear at the head of many chapters. We are cautioned that some of these adages may not have been voiced originally by Harry, but then he is the man who also said, "Originality is undiscovered plagiarism."

DWAYNE HUNN, who could well have authored this book but for the press of other pursuits. The series of articles entitled *Every Town Needs a Castle* which he wrote for the *Glendoran* were invaluable source material and are true literary treasures. Visiting with Dwayne and reminiscing about the early days at the Castle provided much of the enthusiasm for this project.

DORCHEN FORMAN, Michael's sister, for the wealth of material and photographs from the early years which she provided for this work. She is responsible for preserving much of the family photographs, correspondence and newspaper articles which make up the Rubel legacy.

NADINE STRANGE, who so conscientiously edited this manuscript and provided unqualified moral support during the entire project. Time and again she would rescue the author when the computer refused to follow his vague or unintelligible instructions. Nadine's invaluable contributions cannot be adequately acknowledged.

And finally, TED SHEPHERD, whose humor permeated the Castle, its residents and all who came there to lend their efforts. He exemplifies the spirit of camaraderie that made Rubelia the place everyone wanted to be during the decades of construction.

INTRODUCTION

Mention the world-renowned Hearst Castle and visions of opulence and splendor are instantly invoked for most people. But who has ever heard of the Kingdom of Rubelia and its castle? What would someone have done who harbored the same dream as Hearst but lacked the financing to accomplish such a feat? Obviously, he would have needed imagination, resourcefulness and a sense of humor to supplant the essential funding for such a project. This is the intriguing history of events that answers those questions. It is the tale of the Rubel Castle.

The Castle is secluded in the corner of North Live Oak and Palm Drive in Glendora, California, and yet somehow completely dominates this residential neighborhood. It is not reminiscent of those constructed in England and the rest of Europe. It has even less in common with the magnificent edifice on the coast of California built by William Randolph Hearst with untold millions of dollars of imported walls, facades, ceilings, fixtures and art. No, this Castle in the Kingdom of Rubelia is the stuff of dreams. It is more a tribute to the imagination and determination of one man and his friends.

The Castle itself defies the ordinary person's imagination and challenges description; for it is a physical embodiment of the lifelong dream of Michael Rubel and the support of a community which both participated in the dream and yet defied him to build it. Once fully viewed, explored, understood and appreciated for the richness of its legacy, it is etched in memory along with the great castles of the world. For this is a monument to a man, his love of and joy in life, his friends and the limitless potential which even today pervades this land.

The challenge presented by any attempt to relate the entire tale of the events which brought this project to fruition is tantalizing. It is one thing to experience the Castle and its residents, but entirely another to reduce it to words which adequately reflect the spirit which brought about its creation. Michael's response when I first proposed this attempt was typical, "It would be great if you want to try and make sense of this chaos." The flavor which the Castle brings to the neighborhood was best captured by a neighbor who wrote the following for the *Glendoran* Magazine in March of 1995:

> For 17 years I have looked out my kitchen window onto a massive wood-hewn gate that slowly and electronically opens and shuts. Above the gate is a hand-welded arch of metal that lacelike spells out the name 'Rubel Farms.' Not only is the gate intriguing but the rock castle rising above the high cinder block walls stirs the imagination also. This is the estate of the lovable, eccentric Michael Rubel. Although Rubel is a friendly type, he likes his privacy, hence the fortress-like gate.

> At times this mysterious Castle Gate slowly opens and in go droves of Senior Citizens for a covered dish potluck dinner. Again it opens slowly to entirely different-style guests who park their antique motorcycles and enter to party. Fifty or so antique cars may enter and exit through this gate when Michael puts on a parade or has a car rally. One morning there were men standing every fifty feet or so along the Castle wall and one near my door. Prince Phillip walked through the gate. A red car pulled up to the drive into the gate with a license

that reads 'DUSTY'…..It was Dustin Hoffman of course. When I told my husband that a full-sized Santa Fe caboose went over the gate one morning, he smiled and said, 'Yes dear.' I know how it feels to be across the street from Samantha and Darren in the old T.V. series called *Bewitched*. The gate is opening now and I hear Rubel's red tractor putt-putting out the castle gate. Typical farmer with his straw hat and farmer-john overalls he has two faithful dogs following closely behind. Mike stops at each home on our cul-de-sac and delivers three or four avocados for each neighbor and disappears back past the gate into the privacy of his castle.

By far the most enthusiastic visitors are the many school buses loaded with children from as far away as Palm Springs coming for their annual tour of the farm and beautifully restored Santa Fe caboose. His desire is to let the students know where train men lived, ate, slept, bathed… on their cross country routes.

Often the gate swings wide for the hay truck to deliver bales of hay for the horses. The geese may decide to take a gander at the outside world and waddle out onto Live Oak Avenue causing drivers to stop and give them the right of way.

The huge Easter egg rock which I am told weighs about 12 tons, hosts people practically every day who stand on top trying to see over the wall. My husband, when working outside, is often asked,

'What is that place?' His answer to many people makes us laugh.

Mr. Rubel graciously has tours scheduled from time to time to allow visitors from all over the world to have a guided tour and take home pictures of the crusader towers, clock tower, working windmill and a huge swing in an ancient oak tree that guarantees even grandmas a flashback to their childhood days.

Life was never dull in my kitchen and looking across the way I could always see some unusual thing happening at what I call my Castle Gate. My husband and I have moved and I miss this gate more than anyone can imagine. Our family is thankful for our years in Glendora, across the street from the 'Glendora Pharm' and are so pleased to be returning for our son's wedding inside the Castle Gate.

Ellen Singleton

The reaction of school children who visit the Castle is usually awe and wonderment. That of the adults is much less predictable. A recent letter from a young visitor puts this dichotomy into focus:

"Thank you for showing us the Kastle. It is neet. My name is Jim. I am in Mrs. Bollingers class. She is nice. My favurat thing was the cabus (caboose). My mother came with our class. She thinks the castle stinks. She says gussus (geese) should not be in the house. She says the chikens shud be outside to. Thank you for letting us cume.   Jimmy"

The "Castle" is more than just a unique structure. It is symbolic of a way of life, a community which is founded on fellowship, and a spirit which cuts across generations and epitomizes humanity. It is also more than the Castle itself, for the entire compound outside of its walls is home to many other equally unique buildings, structures, adornments and human activity. This fascinating blend of architecture and human interaction has caused the name "Rubel Pharms" to be commonly used to describe the place. The term was first used by Michael's friend, Ted Shepherd, and it was so descriptive that it stuck. People also began to refer to this adult Disneyland as the "Kingdom of Rubelia" and Michael as the "Lord of Rubelia."

Although much has been written and disseminated about this modern day phenomenon, and though it has been visited by notable personages from all over the world, the story deserves to be told in depth for it reaffirms our faith in the joy of living and the immortality of the whimsical spirit.

ONE

The Castle

"Michael's perception of reality is
not quite adequate."

Harry Deuel, Michael's
maternal grandfather

The inevitable comment heard from every visitor to the Castle is, "It's really impossible to describe this." There's a compelling reason for such commentary. The Castle is a voyage into the unknown, a venture into the deepest and darkest reaches of the imagination. Perhaps if you were to meet the King and Queen of Rubelia, the name which is often affectionately assigned to this most unusual asterisk in the world of royal domains, you would be better prepared to comprehend its charm and nobility. Michael is known as the King or Lord of Rubelia, and his personality and enthusiasm will provide you with some insight into the mixture of magnificence and inane, the real and the imaginary, and the sublime and the ridiculous which pervade the Castle and its grounds.

Approaching the Castle site on Live Oak provides little hint of what lies ahead. The tree-lined streets and attractive homes, with the rugged San Gabriel Mountains as a backdrop, give a comfortable feeling of security and serenity. The first indication that you are encountering something unusual is the eight-foot cinder block wall surrounding the two and one-half acre tract in which the Castle is located. A massive and imposing wood and steel gate bears a sign reading, "Rubelia." Many beautiful palm,

1

eucalyptus, elm, avocado, orange, lemon and numerous other trees rise above the wall and the impression would be of a lingering rural area inside the city; except for the apex of the Castle towers rising above the wall and trees. Entering the large gate projects you into a new world for which your experiences have not prepared you.

The senses are assaulted immediately upon viewing the Castle exterior wall which is circular. It arises out of its initial foundation, a concrete reservoir one hundred eighty-five feet in diameter, with walls two feet thick and eighteen feet high. The interior and exterior walls, in fact the entire castle itself, have been completely laminated with a siding composed of hundreds of thousands of tons of large river rock set in concrete, leaving the structure bearing no resemblance to the original reservoir. A second glance at the walls brings the realization that the notion of nobility here, like every other attempt to stratify mankind, has a very distinct chink in its armor. For protruding from the concrete mortar part of an old motorcycle is observed, then a well-worn laborer's glove of one of the volunteer workers, an old toaster, a golf club, wine bottles, a musical instrument, hay hooks, pipes, old machine parts, spy cameras, and on and on. Was this a serious attempt to erect a castle for the twentieth century to take pride in, or was it a flight into an imaginary world that only the child in us can understand? Despite the enormity of the castle structure, the symmetry of its lines and the graceful placement of the towers and castle workshops, the suspicion intrudes that we are not fully realizing what its creator had in mind.

Michael Clarke Rubel, the owner, architect, builder and very spirit of the Castle only seems to see the humor and joy in living, without a thought to creating a monument to his genius and a legacy for his family. But this is a man who is deep and philosophical beneath his cheerful and friendly demeanor. So you may be left wondering; is this Castle a gigantic practical joke or is it the fulfillment of the dream of a real visionary? Michael answers the question posed with typical ambiguity, "I would rather build my forts and castles; besides it keeps me off the streets. Everyone has to have something wrong with them. When I first started, everyone said I was crazy. When I put up the fortress-like walls, they called me eccentric, so you see I am improving myself." But despite his disclaimers and irrespective of his motivation in bringing Rubelia into existence, he has created a lasting memorial to his own individuality and the humorous and whimsical nature of mankind. He has also accomplished a very complex and innovative construction that many would say was impossible.

A massive double draw gate, constructed of vertical timbers and bound with wrought iron supports and edging, guards the tunnel-like entrance to the castle compound itself. Naturally, the gate is electronically operated and this imposing ingress into the grounds has been aptly described by Richard Macy, a long-time friend of Michael's and a volunteer Castle docent, as something straight from the "Munsters." The impression as you enter through this dark passageway is of leaving behind the world as you know it and entering the world as Michael knows it.

Emerging into the Castle enclosure is almost a disorienting experience, of being assailed with massive concrete and rock walls implanted with multiple towers rising to seventy or more feet in this circular enclave. The towers each have their own dedicated purpose and individuality; one houses an historic 1890 weight-driven, hand wound Seth Thomas clock with working chimes (more about this in a later chapter), another boasting battlements and cannon, presumably protecting the Castle from that other world, and still another with a giant bronze bell reached by narrow and precipitous circular stairs from the castle floor to the top. The towers boast of a time before OSHA and similar agencies began trying to live our lives vicariously. They dominate the Castle courtyard and are really only fully visible from this vantage point since the many trees and walls protect the entire castle compound from the outside world.

The Castle grounds inside these circular walls are still another element of the time warp you have entered. In the center stands a castle shop of the inevitable rock construction with an enormous circular wooden beam and shingle roof. It houses fully equipped and operational blacksmith and machine shops. The unique tools are reminders of earlier times, classic in design and some of inestimable value. The Castle blacksmith is Warren Asa, a retired horticulturalist, who still practices and teaches that almost forgotten trade at the Castle. You will find that Michael's world is inhabited by such people as Warren, all fascinating, multi-talented and willing to give of their time to the continuance of this most unusual domain. A stained glass shop, weaving chamber and printing shop with old hand presses and hand-set type, again all fully functional and of antiquarian design, inhabit other chambers built into the castle walls.

Absorbing the panorama around the castle courtyard one gets the first hint of why Michael's sister, Dorchen, once remarked, "Mike's sole purpose in life is to keep anything from going to the dump." Although typically a comment to be expected from an older sister, the uninitiated may find the same idea formulating upon the first sight of the expanse strewn with old machines, mining rail cars and track, engines, propane canons for holiday excitement, very old tractors, pumps, cement mixer and antique machinery which can only be described and deified by

4

Michael, who has a special place in his heart for every piece of junk/treasure which has found a home there. One of the more unique items in the courtyard is a life-sized "Tin Man" wearing a welding mask and holding a stinger. It was a gift from a friend who had asked his wife for a welder for Christmas. He was not amused that she had spent more having the "Tin Man" welder made than the welder itself subsequently cost. This is just another part of the comic relief which suggests that you not take anything here too seriously.

To the more practical-minded person, the entire two and one-half acre compound surrounding the Castle may appear to justify Dorchen's observation, but almost every item has unique value, if not by conventional appraisal then in the story of its acquisition or its original usage. But don't be misled, there are countless pieces which are irreplaceable and together they form a history and priceless lore that will be explored in more detail in later chapters. And yes, the geese, chickens and dogs are wandering through the castle courtyard and grounds; but not in the living premises, where even shoes are not allowed.

Michael never intended the Castle to be anything but his home, and the stairs to the second story living quarters are anything but a regal entrance. The steep, steel steps rising from the courtyard are guarded by a pipe handrail. A protruding, covered porch and walkway lead to the entrance of Michael and Kaia's home. Quite in keeping with the maze of electronic gadgets throughout the Castle and surrounding grounds, passing a certain point on this walkway triggers a wolf whistle and alerts residents to approaching visitors. Only when shoes are removed may entrance be gained. Construction of this portion of the Castle began with the placement of lengths of railroad tracks in the castle floor as the basic support for residence walls facing the courtyard, with the opposite walls being the reservoir wall. The rail tracks were strengthened with steel cables from the old Morris Dam in Glendora and then, inevitably, finished with more river rock and concrete mortar. Interestingly, very little of the construction materials for the entire castle were purchased. Much was donated, scavenged and salvaged from certain deterioration or the dump. Many claim that Rubel was a recycler before anyone even knew what the word meant. Dwayne Hunn, one of Michael's friends and one of the original group helping to build the Castle recalled those early times in an article in the *Glendoran* in 1991:

> Only two years remained before the hip decade of the sixties would be history. Five of us with two decades of experience under our belts were living on a two and one half acre 'pharm' where piles of railroad ties were stacked and tottering 15 and 20 feet into the air. Neighbors left bags of bottles in the driveway, rocks and tunnel beams - taken from the Los Angeles Feather River project via the Pharm's rattling 22 year old flatbed truck – were strewn here and there on the acreage. We knew the 'collected junk' was to build memorable stuff and Michael's dream – A CASTLE MADE OF LEFTOVERS. Unfortunately, the ritzy suburban neighborhood didn't have the same confident vision, imagination or sense of foolhardiness.

> For the five of us, there probably never was or could be a better home for that time, or maybe any time, of our lives. For me at least, I don't believe there could have been any better place to live. On the other hand, the expensive surrounding

suburban neighbors felt our home was just a bigger than life 'Sanford and Son' backyard that made their eyes sore and dispositions sour.

Today, with a lot of help from his friends, luck and the good Lord, Michael and gang have buried most of that 'collected junk' and other treasures within the walls of the seven and a half story Rubelian Castle Made of Leftovers. Some of the collected junk became windmills made of retired telephone poles. Some of the railroad ties became the walls of my old house. Some of the siding from old barns and wineries became house walls, castle ceilings and firewood. All of the neighbors' recycled bottles sit in the walls of the castle, sometimes reflecting their varied colors to the outside world when the 13 pharm fireplaces work their sparkles.

They say that if you put enough monkeys in front of enough typewriters long enough, you can get the Bible written. If you have enough people pile junk together often enough, I reckon you can build a castle.

The living area consists of cramped but charming rooms between these two walls, usually connected by catwalks, some of which are open to the castle floor itself. The ceilings are low and the rooms; office, kitchen, bathroom, bedrooms, living room with antique ham radio equipment, and pool room, all have old wooden walls, Italian ceramic tile floors and both electrical and lantern lighting. The array of antiques and unconventional furnishings is more than stunning and one seems to be taken back hundreds of years in time.

It is at once apparent that the kitchen is really the social center where friends gather. Cooking is done on a 1910 Crawford Century woodstove with porcelain finish that is burning constantly in the winter months and provides heat for the living area. Mike boasts that he can properly stoke and vent this stove to produce a perfect 350 degree oven for baking. Old copper and iron pots and pans and utensils hang from the ceiling and the preparation table and counter are of antique and well-used wood variety. Meals are served and eaten on a wooden board balanced on your lap since there is no room for a table, and since such modern conveniences would detract from the style and symmetry of the quarters. As the woodstove also heats the water for the residents, the wood supply must be replenished daily.

Each room exudes its own special charm and more than compensates for the absence of modern conveniences. It is true that the office boasts a computer and the kitchen a television, but these are more anomalies than typical. The Rubels' bedroom has an antique bed and dresser and a sword from another era hanging on the wall. There is also a cabinet there with a collection of antique Winchester rifles, a gift from Michael's grandfather. The pool room is dominated by a beautiful Arden pool table of exquisite design which was assembled on site and is perfectly balanced. Windows all face from the rooms into the courtyard, but there is only enough light so as not to detract from the medieval character of the interior. In fact, there is a certain enchantment here which can never be defined or elucidated. It can only be experienced by entering into the world of Rubelia.

Embarking into this world demands that you put aside all notion of the practical and the serious, for here there seems to be a realization that our dreams are only equaled in importance by our friends. Michael Rubel has adopted a formula for living which is not for everyone, but the degree to which it is embraced seems to enhance our appreciation of life and our very humanity. Who is this man who can inspire such admiration for doing nothing more than that which he wanted during his life, who follows his dreams with a determination that refuses to recognize barriers? Where did this man come from and what set him on a course for a life so unusual and so fun-filled and work-filled that he becomes an object of admiration? Michael will deny that this admiration exists; in fact, he claims that his insurance man blames him for being an alcoholic because of many of the obviously dangerous stairways, passageways and ledges in the Castle. But the fact remains that he is a truly charismatic person to all who meet him, except of course, those who may have been frustrated by the single-mindedness of his pursuits.

We will attempt to explore some of the history, the humor, the struggles and the spirit which inspired this man and his friends. Perhaps the journey will answer some of the questions posed, but more likely it will engender more questions and speculation. One may come to suspect that Michael, with his ever-present smile, would have you believe that there are no answers; and if there were, they wouldn't be of any importance, and might not even be the truth.

TWO

The Embryonic Years

"With that kind of background, you'd hardly
expect me to be normal."

Michael Rubel

Imagine a mother who had been a chorus girl in New York
and who had danced in the famous Ziegfield Follies. Who had
sung with her sister as the Deuel Sisters and were headlined for
five years in the roaring twenties on the Broadway stage with such
legendary stars as Fanny Brice, Oscar Shaw, Grace Moore and
Jack Benny. Who had a collection of over two thousand gowns
dating from 1835 and a collection of hats sufficient to allow her to
wear several a day for every day of the year and still have
countless left over. Who counted the famous fan dancer, Sally
Rand, as one of her closest friends and was the most celebrated
hostess in Southern California, organizing magnificent parties for
almost any occasion, often for local philanthropic causes.

Imagine a father who was an Episcopalian minister and a
gag writer under contract with Paramount Pictures. Who wrote
skits for vaudeville and later penned songs and scripts for the radio
comedian Joe Penner, for whom he coined the well-known line,
"Wanna buy a duck?" Who was appointed Rector of the Grace
Episcopal Church in Glendora, a position he held until his death in
1946. Who in 1938 sought community support to change the name
of Glendora to "The Little Town of Bethlehem." Who drew
visitors from all over Southern California when he preached at the
Church, beginning his homily with a series of jokes and humorous

stories and then turning to more serious spiritual matters. Who might then conclude his presentation in a very reverent tone: "We might have been lighthearted, but on this day of worship and prayer we should always remember, 'Wanna buy a duck?'"

Imagine a father and mother who did a radio show under the name of Hal and Dorothy Raynor for many years, as well as a radio show as King and Queen Kill Kare on the National Biscuit NBC show. Who were two of the most kindly, dynamic and beloved people known to their friends in Glendora.

Not exactly your ordinary family! Now imagine being the third and youngest child of such parents, born after the family had relocated in Glendora from New York in 1936. Michael's roots seem to have predisposed him for a life filled with equal parts of fun and fantasy. Although his father died when he was only six, he did not lack for guidance from older friends. The most significant was Odo Stade who lived next door to the Rubels and, "had the most profound influence on my life. He was a good, honest, straightforward man, extremely hardworking, proud and decent." Recalls Michael, "Odo became my father figure. A boy couldn't have had a better one. He was very generous and patient with the questions of a small boy. I remember our many camping trips. He was the most fascinating man I've ever known."

Stade was an excellent choice for a substitute father, having been named "Citizen of the Year" in Glendora in 1956, and being a renowned scholar. He studied law and economics at the University of Vienna, graduating at the age of fifteen. Mr. Stade traveled over much of the world and was inducted into the Austro-Hungarian Navy in 1912 as a navigator. He was a published author and with E. Pinchon wrote the biography, *Viva Villa*, which eventually became a motion picture. It does not require a stretch of the

11

imagination to understand how this man, who was fluent in sixteen languages, occupied such a prominent role in Michael's life. It also introduces a further element of complexity into the character of this man/boy who supposedly never grew up and lived to build his castles.

An interesting segment of Odo Stade's life was destined to become a part of Michael's fascinating legacy. While in the Austro-Hungarian navy during a voyage, the crew mutinied and ordered Odo to set a course for California. The year was 1915 and the maps that were available to them did not distinguish between California and Baja California. Odo's calculations brought the ship to land on the Baja peninsula, where they were met by Pancho Villa and his band of rebels. They shot the first two men who debarked from the ship because they did not like their attitude. Odo Stade had put on a French military strategist officer's uniform, which was in the ship's trunk. He left the ship expecting to be shot, when Villa asked through an interpreter what uniform he was wearing. Being then fluent in Spanish and six other languages, Odo answered the rebel directly in excellent Spanish that he was wearing a military strategist's uniform. Villa was impressed with his command of the language and ordered that Stade would be his military strategist since he did not have one. Of course, Odo knew nothing of military strategy but had no choice other than to comply.

Mr. Stade spent the next eight years, from 1915 to 1923 serving Villa's revolutionary forces. Although he did not like Villa or his methods, he knew any attempt to escape would result in the revolutionaries hunting him down and killing him. Odo was present at Villa's ranch when a big black car pulled up in the front yard. When Villa approached the car he was machine-gunned to death. Stade was in the back of the house and heard the shots.

Shortly thereafter he switched boots with Villa since his were in very poor condition. He also purchased Villa's Colt 45 long barrel pistol from another of the rebels a short time later. He was able to escape soon thereafter, but not before sustaining three serious gunshot wounds in his chest. Today, those boots and Villa's pistol are in Michael's safe, a gift from Stade on his fifteenth birthday. There is compelling documentation for the authenticity of the gun and Michael has refused a substantial offer for it, a memento from Odo being far too valuable to part with.

Stade came to Southern California in 1923 and ran a bookstore until the Depression. The remainder of his career was spent in the Forest Service while residing in Glendora. His picture occupies a special place in Michael's Castle bedroom, along with another gift from Odo, a Seth Thomas clock which is over one hundred years old.

Dorothy Rubel was obviously the other pervasive influence in her son's life. She was eulogized after her death in 1977 by her social secretary from 1967 to 1977, Marion Ashby, "As a gifted hostess she not only enjoyed entertaining her friends but made her home and talents available to numerous organizations and groups. It was, however, in her personal relationships with individuals that her greatest services were done. Tolerant and accepting of people in their weaknesses as well as their strengths, she made each of her friends feel, 'Like a special friend.' She was a lady with a loving heart."

When the Rubel family arrived in Glendora in 1936, the Reverend Henry Scott Rubel, affectionately called, "Heinz," by almost everyone, became Pastor of the Grace Episcopal Church. Dorothy had been a star in New York and brought an element of glamour to this small town in Southern California, which then had a population of just over a thousand people. Glendora was never to be the same thereafter! Until that time it had been a sleepy community where you knew your mailman and his family and he, in turn, knew all about yours.

Dorothy began giving large, elegant parties with guests sometimes numbering over a thousand, including such notables as Bob Hope, Jack Benny, Edward G. Robinson, Alfred Hitchcock, Frankie Walrus the Keystone Kop and countless others. Often her close friend and neighbor, Sally Rand, who had gained fame internationally, would perform her tantalizing fan dance for the guests. "These parties were given for almost any reason." Richard Macy recalls, "There were birthday parties, graduation parties, coming out parties, going away parties, wedding parties, promotion and demotion parties and Hawaiian luaus. When she couldn't find a reason for a party, she just had a party-party."

When you were a guest at one of Dorothy's parties you had definitely "arrived." There were almost never small parties because guests would inevitably ask to bring friends or out of town guests and the size of the party would grow exponentially. But Dorothy would always warmly embrace everyone into the festivities. "Whenever mother would want to have a small party," Michael relates, "she would wait until the night before to extend her invitations so as not to give her guests time to 'spread the word'. This worked sometimes, but it is amazing how some of those ladies worked their telephones and mother was often surprised by greater numbers than she anticipated."

The impression that Dorothy was just a "hostess extraordinaire," as she was called by many, should be emphatically dispelled. Her aptitude for business became apparent when Heinz' death required her to become the sole support of the family. She was equally talented and successful in her commercial pursuits. She established a successful career as a realtor and was referred to as "The Lady with Lots" and also briefly was a partner in a retail business known as "Glendorable Goods." Dorothy was a very dynamic woman who had been actively encouraged as a child to pursue activities in which she had an interest, as well as being provided the tools to do so. Certainly this encouragement found its place in Michael's life as well, and the notion that dreams could be pursued and attained never seems to have been questioned.

Michael's mother was beloved by everyone with whom she came into contact. She was always ready to help everyone whose life she touched, as well as contributing energetically to community projects. She seems to typify the spirit which has become an integral part of the community ever since she began infusing life into it in 1936. When she was dying of cancer in 1977, Michael recalls that, "Several people came to visit her who had not paid her in earlier years for real estate transactions she had handled for them. They brought checks for the amount they owed her and apologized for their tardiness, expressing disbelief that she had still counted them among her friends and included them at her parties. She had dismissed their concerns and said that it did not affect her regard for them."

Dorothy may have had a more immediate influence on the life path that her son chose. His sister, Dorchen, remembers that, "He started building forts when he was four years old because Mother kept saying to him, 'Go outside and play.' The poor, homeless waif had to build himself a home!" The Rubels lived near a junkyard on the outskirts of Glendora and Michael and his friends loved building forts and castles there. There was an endless supply of junk for this endeavor and most likely produced the reverence which Mike has harbored ever since for the old and

15

the discarded. Michael's friends, Skipper Landon, David Wilson, Duncan Menser and John McHann joined in this activity and John McHann's son, Jason, recalls that one of their buildings was so high that one of their mothers made them put up a fire escape. "They were so good at building that pictures appeared in *Life* magazine in 1954," Jason tells us.

The boyhood forts and castles were far from ordinary. The first one or two were experimental in nature and bore a resemblance to the playhouses which any eight or nine year old might build out of old scrap lumber and packing cases. But Michael's vision reached out to pinnacles far beyond the imagination of the normal youth. Soon his castles were to attain a height of sixty-five feet, encompass fourteen rooms, cannons, a cook stove and fire pit, and a drawbridge for access over the moat. They had an endless supply of aluminum nails for the project, called "Skipper nails," which Mr. Landon acquired when he was working for Alcoa Aluminum. The boys maintained the stability of these "skyscrapers" against the force of the Santa Ana Winds with guy wires to the surrounding orange and pine trees. It was not uncommon for them to spend months on one of these building projects, which even then put them out of favor with City Officials.

These childhood fortresses were featured in a children's book written by Michael's uncle, Harry A. Deuel, Jr., *Castles By Mike*, which was published in 1966. The opening page of the text quoting Michael was prophetic for it set a tone for his life:

"I'm Mike. I build Castles.

Everybody dreams of castles now and then, but I build 'em. I'd like the chance to be your General Contractor when you decide you really want to build one.

Let me show you some pictures I took of my work. I think you'll agree I have to be one the most experienced castle builder anywhere around, these days. Experience is important in a project of this nature."

Most of us put these childhood fantasies behind us in the process of trying to conform to society's "norms." But some part of the ten-year old Michael refused to grow with the rest of him. He must have possessed a sense of something that is timeless in all of us, and had the capacity to enrich our lives far more than conforming. It was even then apparent that the cannons and towers reaching to the sky were an integral part of the reality which Michael knew, or more correctly, chose for himself."

"Michael was a 'free spirit' at a very early age." Skipper Landon's mother, Florence, contends. "I remember him using a piece of railing from our home in 1951 in one of his castles, and it's pictured in the children's book, *Castles by Mike*," a volume which now can be found in the Glendora Library. It was even then apparent that Michael was being propelled toward a life that was centered around his imagination, his friends and the notion of unlimited fun. One of his long-time friends, Nick Moffitt, who is Mike's 'look-alike', confirms that the Castle is more than just a structure; it is also a state-of-mind which began long ago and still persists:

In the early days I was goaded into shenanigans by the older pharm hands. I guess I was about five years old and really looked up to my big pharm brothers. I'd talk my mother into dropping me off at Michael Rubel's place, amidst the orange groves. I convinced her to get rid of me, for days at a time. There were always a bunch of kids doing creative things. We built tunnels: we built forts (incredible forts that no one could comprehend today). We played on his World War I cannon. We hiked up the Dalton Wash into the foothills. What adventures we had!

One of these memorable adventures was greasing the Pacific Electric Red Car tracks in the center of Glendora. Mr. Frank 'Red' Sisson would let us keep the old grease we cleaned up after cars were lubed at his Flying A station. The bigger kids, like Klaus Schilling, Skipper Landon, Charles something or other, and this guy named Michael, would allow me to help them with their civic projects. One project was smearing grease on the Red Car tracks. When the Red Car would try to stop at the station on the east side of Glendora Avenue (formerly Michigan Avenue), it smoothly slid all the way down to what is now called Finkbiner Park. You should have seen the expressions on the faces of the trolley operator and passengers. They thought the brakes had failed. It was absolutely priceless.

It was a small town in those days with every one knowing each other. It reminds me of the saying we hear today, 'it takes a village to raise children.'

All this may be only representative of how most kids grew up in those days. Why should Michael alone pursue a childhood goal throughout adult life? The answer may lie in another dominating influence in his early life. Glendora had until the middle of the twentieth century been a town completely dependent on the citrus industry. That fact was true of much of Southern California; remember that Disneyland was originally a beautiful orange grove. Glendorans were totally dependent on the vitality of the citrus groves and the growers depended on the townspeople for all of their needs. A record freeze hit the area in January of 1949, with temperatures dropping as low as twenty- three degrees. Oranges would freeze at twenty-eight degrees and smudge pots were burning for ten and fifteen hours at a time, resulting in energy shortages and wildly fluctuating citrus prices. The entire economy of the area was in jeopardy.

Close to the Rubel home was another of Michael's favorite retreats as a youth – the Albourne citrus ranch, which had originally been called the Dalton Rancho. Arthur K. Bourne, the owner, was the Singer Sewing Machine magnate and had named the ranch after his wife, Alberta. The ranch was a perfect playground for Mike and his friends for it boasted a very large reservoir (now the Castle) which became the summer swimming hole for the youths. The ranch had a very large citrus packing plant and many other ranch buildings in addition to the orange groves.

"If Mr. Bourne saw us (swimming) he would tell us to get out because we might get hurt, drowned, polio or whatever else popped into his head," said Michael. "But I was always his buddy as a kid and I kept telling him that when I grew up I wanted to buy the reservoir and the packing house." The ranch became a second home to Michael and even after the economy took its toll and the ranch closed in 1949, it remained his favorite place. Mr. Bourne continued to live in Glendora until 1954, but the ranch and its buildings became neglected and deteriorated as a result of being unoccupied for so many years. Windows were broken by vandals, and Michael even confesses to having shot out a few himself. But the ranch was later to become the most important influence in Michael's early life.

The experiences with school during these same years were not as satisfying for Michael. Undoubtedly, the discipline and structure were foreign to the life he had been living. Dorothy had allowed him complete freedom from a very early age. "She was so busy working and trying to make a living for us that she really didn't have time to supervise me and, besides, I was having the time of my life and not getting into any real trouble. I had a very happy childhood and Mother was content to let me be," Michael reflects. The family was quite poor after Heinz' death in 1946, when Michael was six, and often he would go to the Landon's house and go into the refrigerator to get food. "I don't think Mrs. Landon liked it too much, but she never said anything to me. A few close friends also gave my mother money during this period until she became more established in the real estate business."

Dorothy's preoccupation with making a living at this time was certainly a critical factor in the freedom which Michael enjoyed, a freedom which has undoubtedly been an important contributor to the unbounded joy with which he views life and his friends. "It was a marvelous time in my life," Michael relates, "Glendora was very small then and we all had guns and could do whatever we wanted." Skipper's mother once said to Dorothy, "You should discipline that boy sometimes. I can't have Skipper running around with Michael, they're always doing something strange."

"I think he was just meant to live," was Dorothy's revealing reply.

Frank "Skipper" Landon did not need Michael to entice him into strange activities. He was very creative in his own right, and was an endless source of ideas for new adventures. A good example is the time the two boys were in the Landon living room and Skipper told Michael he could make a machine gun out of a Daisy BB gun. The inventive ten-year-old soldered a small nipple to the base of the barrel and connected it with tubing and clamps to a fire extinguisher. The fact that the extinguisher was under 2000 pounds per square inch of pressure did not seem important to the inventors who were only impressed with the fact that the BB gun held about a hundred BB's in the chamber. Skipper had Michael hold the extinguisher and told him to open the valve slowly. The experiment worked. When the valve was opened slowly, the BB's were spewed out under great pressure all over the living room, breaking windows and ornate vases on the mantel. Florence was furious and promised Skipper a beating when his father got home. "Michael opened the valve," was the best defense he could muster.

Michael went from one school to another for most of those years, usually never lasting more than three or four months before being expelled; well, not really expelled, but the headmaster would call his mother and tell her that it was not working out well and she should find another school. He claims he absolutely hated school and, as many of them were away from home, he would always miss his dogs. Usually, his ingenuity figured out a way to get him back home again.

He variously attended the Harding Military Academy in the canyon north of Glendora, the Norton School in Claremont, the Wilson school in Glendora, a public school which he absolutely loved because "they let us do whatever we wanted," the Midland School in the Santa Ynez Valley, Citrus High School and the Jesuit-run Don Bosco. The latter was a better experience because they taught him electronics, a discipline which has always served him well.

The Midland School experience is typical of the path that Michael's educational history followed. Midland was in the Santa Ynez Valley near Santa Barbara on a tract of land encompassing 36,000 acres, which has since been split into smaller parcels. One such parcel is now the locale for Michael Jackson's home. Midland was a British school owned by the Squibb family (the pharmaceutical company) and was a strictly run academy housed in very rustic conditions with no electricity. Michael was in the Phoenix House and he and his roommates would often go through the rough wooden floor at night and build tunnels for fun. The school had a regimen which required that if certain daily grades were not attained, the student was required to go to study hall that afternoon, for fully three or four hours.

Michael was often required to go, but soon figured out that the Headmaster was bothered by his being on the detention list. So Michael intuitively realized he had an edge and decided to go every afternoon whether required or not. The Headmaster would ask him why he was there and Michael would respond that he needed to get good grades and he had to go. The Headmaster responded, "Well, your grades are okay."

"Oh no, I have to get better grades."

Exasperated, the Headmaster said he didn't want him coming to study hall any more.

"Well I have to, sir, because I have to get A's."

At his wits' end the Headmaster finally said, "You'll *never* get A's, Michael!"

He finally called Dorothy and suggested that he be sent to Don Bosco, saying that Michael was, technically, incredibly competent but scholastically very poor because of his attitude. An interesting sidelight is that years later when Michael's nephew, Scott Rubel, was a student at Midland in 1969, heavy rains caused flooding and the collapse of the tunnels under Phoenix House and the school's reaction was, "That's damn Michael Rubel's work."

Rubel was pleased with the vocational side of the education at Don Bosco but was less than impressed with the religious indoctrination. This school had a policy of accepting non-Catholic students and would operate as a non-sectarian institution, but in practice they would always find a way of introducing Catholic doctrine in "Ethics" classes. This drove Michael, "literally bananas" and he began reminding his teachers of the Crusades, the religious persecutions and the earlier Popes fathering children. When he started espousing the teachings of Voltaire and documenting the Popes' indiscretions, the Principal said, "Michael, you're so disruptive, I can't have you come to school here next year."

"Oh great, your damn religion's the most god awful thing."

"We don't teach religion here!"

"Oh yes you do!" Michael could not resist a parting shot.

So the educational pattern continued throughout all of the school years. He did attend Citrus High School for one month in order to complete an English requirement and receive a high school diploma. There was nothing regular or conventional about Michael's education, but he is a highly articulate, intelligent and well-read man. The educational system and Michael may seem to have been at war with each other, but it is probably closer to the truth to say that they spoke entirely different languages.

Summers were special times for Michael because there were no expectations of educational achievement. He would often spend most of the season up in the San Gabriel's on the Fricke Ranch. He lived in a bee house and sometimes worked with the bees and in Mr. Fricke's orchards. Dorothy would leave him a carton of food each Monday morning at the foot of the path leading up to the Ranch, and he would collect it later in the day. The life was perfectly suited to Michael's free spirit, for he could carry his guns, sleep on the roof of the bee house and set free his imagination. It was here that he met the Pecks, who were to be another addition to his list of surrogate parents. Sedley "Papa" Peck had been a courier for General Eisenhower during World War II and Flo Flo had been his personal cook. Flo Flo's recollections of Michael in the *Glendoran* echo those of so many others whose paths have crossed his:

> I've known Mike since he was 9 years old. He was a very nice youngster and now he's a very nice man. He's also very ambitious. Though he's a good-hearted man, he can also be very stubborn. Michael very easily could have been born two centuries ago.

Michael was only twelve or thirteen years old when then President Eisenhower was in Southern California and came up to visit the Pecks at their mountain home. The Secret Service preceded the visit with a security check of the whole area. Michael happened to be there at the time, wearing his pistol and carrying a rifle. He remembers, "I didn't even know who Eisenhower was. I was so stupid. I'd heard the name, but……" The Secret Service told him they would have to hold his guns and return them after Eisenhower departed.

"Papa Peck told me never to give my guns to anybody," Michael responded, standing his ground.

"He won't give us his guns," they complained to Mr. Fricke.

"Good for him. Good lesson," Fricke came back, applauding Michael's adherence to principles.

The visit occurred without Michael, who sat on a hill, with his guns, some distance away and watched the entourage approach, his independent spirit still intact.

The times that he was not at school in those years were spent hiking and hopping railroad trains with a buddy, Jim Cook, and traveling to interesting places near and far, from Azusa next door to distant destinations in Arizona and Texas. He and Jim had learned the hobo's life in very early years and even as youths of seven or eight years they had been hopping rides on trains to nearby communities. These activities were much better suited to Michael's free-spirited nature and launched him into the next stage of his life. It should become easier to visualize the kind of person who would passionately throw himself into endeavors that he might choose, but certainly not those that were required or expected of him.

Where do we look to find some insight into a life that seems to have been lived outside of what could be termed ordinary parameters? Michael never kept a journal of any sort, but at infrequent times he would record his inner reflections on his identity and the world as he perceived it. He put such thoughts down on paper on September 15, 1970, and we are indebted to his sister, Dorchen, for preserving this revealing self-profile:

9-14-70 Perhaps no one would really understand. I think that is because of my childhood. My Mother worked and Father died.

That was fine with me because I rather preferred the dump, and with those two out of the way, I pretty much did what I liked. That is the reason, perhaps, that I still do what I like. You know the type. But, I never got much out of hurting anyone, so my doings stuck kind of close to me personally, and did not reach out and touch other people. That might be the reason why some people like me.

The first person to make much sense to me was a farmer across the street. He gave me good solid reasons why gophers had to be caught. Why a knife hurt the trees and why water made people kill one another. He treated me like a people (sic) himself, and that made sense to me when I thought about it in my sand pile, near the wash.

Growing up stuck on me rather hard. It seemed as though people were at the bottom of every bit of trouble. Without people, I got along just fine. Mother understood, I think, and that was why she let me live in the mountains. I got along with the few mountain folks I met, and life was just a matter of passing some time. School people gave Mother a lot of trouble, but, that did not bother me much. She was down in the Town where they could get at her a lot.

Mother kind of lost her courage, after a time, and began to believe people. They all told her what she was doing wrong, and that played ill with her. So, after a time, she contacted the Forest Service, and I was taken home by the Forest Patrolman. It always struck me funny that to keep me in our happy home, I had to be taken home by the Patrolman. Seemed as though everyone else took my life rather seriously, but the old men of my life encouraged me to run away when I could manage it. I had lots of backing from my close friends who knew about society. So I spent several years on the freights going about our great country. Then I went around the world for two years. By the time I got home, no one was willing to monkey with my life, so I built a fort here in the middle of town to keep people out and life is going along real well.

The memorandum provides only a brief glimpse into the complex man we know as Michael Rubel, but it does furnish a starting point for comprehending the motivational forces which operate within his world, and for further understanding the unique paths he has chosen to follow. It challenges us to dismiss preconceptions and explore those paths for ourselves.

The Rubel Family
Christopher, Dorchen, Heinz and Michael in front

An unhappy six-year-old Michael at Halloween

Fort/Castle built by nine-year-old Michael and friends

Michael and Kaia in Pharm Hand attire

Main gate into the Castle courtyard

Castle gate on Live Oak featuring "Rubelia" sign

Gun tower adjacent to entryway

Entryway porch to Castle living quarters

Tin Palace main hall

Bedroom in cooling box in Tin Palace

The Bottle House, the first of the Castle structures

The "Tin Man" welder on the Castle floor

THREE

Travels with Michael

"My mother wanted me to be an attorney, but after
flunking out of my first semester of college, I came
to the conclusion that it would be sheer nonsense
for me to try to make a success of my life."

Michael

At eighteen years of age, castles were the furthest thing
from Michael's mind or imagination. The lure of mysterious
faraway places and hidden adventure were beckoning after the
frustrations of education. With a passport and very little money in
his pocket, Michael set off hitchhiking to Mexico. In 1958,
passports were required to enter Mexico, the tourist pass not
having yet made its appearance. The stay in Mexico was brief for
he met some young travelers with a small aircraft. They flew to
Manchester, Connecticut, where Michael went to visit his aunt. At
one of her parties (This must be a family trait!), he met the Captain
of the "Ryndam," one of the larger cruise ships of the Holland
American Line at that time.

He asked the Captain if he could have a job on the ship.
"Well what can you do?" asked the ship's master. "I can do
anything that takes muscles," was the response that got him a job
in the ship's laundry. When the ship docked in Cork, Ireland,
Michael told the Captain he had a passport and would like to leave
the ship, "although in those days I didn't even know where Ireland
was." The Captain agreed to pick him up the next time they made
port there, but long before that occurred he was on his way

hitchhiking again through France and into Germany. He remained several months in Germany with relatives, the Rieke's, and, "had the most wonderful summer of my life; they were absolutely wonderful to me." But again, wanderlust took over and, having bought a motorcycle, went on to tour Russia, the Baltics and on down through Greece and Italy. From there he got transport with his motorcycle to Morocco. Was Michael's Mother alright with this wandering on his own? "She was fine with all of this, you know, 'he was meant to live,' and I think she was relieved I was out of her hair."

Entering this country in western North Africa, Rubel pulled his motorcycle into a gas station and inquired of the attendant, "Where are the Pyramids, you know, the Egyptian Pyramids?"

"They're three thousand miles away."

"I thought they were in North Africa," Michael countered.

"They are, but North Africa is a big place. They're three thousand miles from here."

"I didn't have a clue," Michael concedes, but that did not deter him.

Still undaunted, he went to the French Embassy to replace his visa, which had been lost, in order to cross Algeria on his way east to the Pyramids. The French officials told him he would need to go to Paris to obtain the required document. This was a disappointing turn of events, but Michael's philosophy, even then as in later days when the Castle presented stumbling blocks, has always been that, "Something will always open up for me."

Going back to France was not even an option at this point and he continued east across Morocco toward the Algerian border. About two hundred yards from the crossing point into Algeria he was told that he would never be able to cross without a visa, and advised to ask a young boy who was nearby for assistance. The boy assured him he could get him into the country. "How much will it cost me?" Michael inquired. When the boy advised it would be $5.00, he wanted to know how he would accomplish this illegal crossing. "I take you down this dirt road and then cross over further down and then back on Highway 1 and then you go on." The diversion worked but Michael was still without a visa.

The following day's journey east on that highway brought a new surprise. Michael was shot in the leg, the bullet then penetrating the motorcycle's gas tank. He had no idea where the shot had come from and hid behind a mound of sand right on the edge of the Mediterranean Sea for almost six hours. Injured and without transportation, fortune again turned Michael's way. A passing fishing boat from Spain was close to shore and noticed his plight. When he explained what had happened, they said they were on their way back to Malaga and would take him with them. When leaving the boat at the port there, Michael was shocked when the crew threw his motorcycle into the bay waters from the stairway to the town plaza. The crew said that Franco, then dictator of Spain, would not allow motorcycles to enter Spain twice without a second permit. "If we get caught bringing the motorcycle into the country without a permit, we get in big trouble."

He was then taken to a small infirmary at a Catholic church where his wound was treated and he was allowed to stay for a few days. "The good people who helped me there," after hearing the story of the motorcycle's demise, "then went down and pulled it out of the water and brought it to a mechanic who agreed to clean it up, repair it and restore it to running condition." "I can't afford all this," Michael informed his new-found benefactors, "but they said they would take care of it." When asked where he planned to go next, "I'm trying to see the Pyramids and then get home," Michael told his Spanish friends. They arranged to get him and his motorcycle on board a ship to Port Oran in Algeria, and as he was still without a visa, the Catholic priest also said he would obtain the document for him, "but when you get to Algeria, go across the country as quickly as you can and get into Tunisia," was the priestly advice he was given.

More adventure awaited him in Algeria, for he met a local man at the port who spoke English and offered Michael the opportunity to stay with his family so that he could practice his English. The hospitality was excellent, but it turned out that the fellow was an Algerian revolutionary fighting against French control of the country. The next morning he proposed to take Michael with him and his cohorts, "to fight the French."

"I didn't even know they were at war with the French. That's how stupid I was," Michael remembers. After assuring them that he would go, but didn't want to shoot or even have a gun, the band of rebels left town and set up an ambush along the road. "How do you know the French are even coming?" Michael asked.

"Oh, we know. We're just going to shoot out the tires of their trucks, but not the men."

"Why do you do that?" Michael wanted to know.

"We just capture them, tell them we'll have a party and show them a good time and then they will desert and join us." That's exactly what happened and provides good evidence of why the French campaign never went very well in Algeria.

Michael then continued his journey on to Constantine, where the authorities informed him that his visa was an illegal one and wanted to know where he had gotten it. After he advised them that the Catholics had obtained it for him in Spain, they wanted to know what he was smuggling. "I'm not smuggling," was Michael's official reply, although, in fact, he had been smuggling and trading small amounts of different currencies to finance his trip. This time fortune turned its back on Michael, and the French sent him to jail in Marseille, France. There he met a Dr. Schleigel, who had previously been the German Ambassador to France. He said he had heard that Michael had been put in jail and wanted to represent him. Having very little money, Michael said he was unable to accept the representation, but Schleigel said it did not matter.

"I'll represent you just because the French are so screwed up," and succeeded in having the case dismissed after convincing the judge that the French did not control most of Algeria and, therefore, could not legally issue visas for that country. The good Doctor then invited Michael to stay at his winery and peach orchard, where, again, "I had a most wonderful time. When the Doctor took me to the port in Marseille to get passage to Tunisia, I discovered when I was aboard ship that he had put $200.00 into my passport." Little doubt can remain that Michael trusts in a destiny which has never failed him, and which he, in turn, never questions. This has been the pattern for his life and it continues even today.

His motorcycle took him through Tunisia, Libya and into Egypt, where he finally saw the Pyramids. The motorcycle was then sold in order to finance further travels, and he boarded a barge south to the border of Sudan and Egypt. From there Michael traveled by train to Port Sudan where he met sailors from an Australian ship, and together they devised a plan to smuggle Michael aboard, conceal him in a lifeboat, and eventually bring him to Australia. This was not something Michael could resist, but it turned out badly. Five minutes after boarding, he was discovered, shackled and sent north by mail boat to Suez. He was then delivered to the U.S. Embassy and given three choices; either lose his passport and return home on a ship, pay his own way home, or go to jail in Egypt, "where you will starve to death because they don't feed you in the jails here."

Michael only had nine dollars at this time and couldn't pay for passage home, so he elected to go to jail, not wanting to give up his passport. "When you get hungry enough, they'll call us and you can then sign this paper, agreeing to go home," the Embassy personnel told him. Michael decided to go to jail because, "the embassies in those days were just awful."

Life in jail was not intolerable, the guards letting him go up to the roof to sleep and providing a police escort to a nearby café to allow him to purchase a meal. There was a price for the latter service, however. Michael was expected to buy the policeman a cup of tea on each visit, a treat costing one cent. Not a bad deal, but soon additional policemen began accompanying him to the café when they learned of the treat he would provide. This was difficult for the prisoner since his meals were costing him five cents and he only had about seven dollars left. By the time they switched to a new café, where the tea cost two cents, he had eight policemen with him, and this large contingent caught the attention

33

of the Captain and crew of the S.S. Barachias. This Dutch ship had docked in Suez and the Captain, C.J. Boggs, was curious why an American had so many policemen with him.

A ship's officer was dispatched to inquire of Michael about his situation, and when the crew was leaving, the same officer asked if he would work on the ship without pay if they were able to obtain his release. Michael readily agreed and Captain Boggs – actually his name was Schmidt, but the nickname had been earned earlier for 'bogging' down' on several occasions – was successful in getting the Embassy to release him into his custody. His unpaid position on the ship was chipping paint, a tedious task that left Michael sore and bleeding. He was an outcast as well, since most of the crew was Spanish and they had no use for him. But after three days of very hard work on board, the crew warmed to him and brought him up with them for lunch and their traditional red wine.

Michael sailed for eighteen months on the Barachias, eventually being paid and moving up to work as cabin boy and then in the ship's mess. These travels took him through Ceylon (now Sri Lanka), Sumatra, Borneo and Java. The ship continued on to the United States and Michael decided it was time to return to Glendora.

His impression had been that C.J. Boggs really did not like him, but he enjoyed the travel and work, and returned to sail with him for a four-month period for each of the next four years. His impression of the Captain's regard for him would prove to be very wrong in the future, and provides yet another example of the charmed life that Michael Rubel lives. It would be a mistake, however, to assume that Michael has nothing to do with the good fortune that meets him at almost every turn. He would probably deny it, but the magnetism of his unassuming personality, the optimism, the goodness of his heart and the work ethic which he exudes, all contribute to his magical path in life.

FOUR

The Beginnings of a Life's Work

"Blessed be our imagination – it makes
life a toy."

Grandfather Deuel

The year was 1959, and the post-World War II economy
was expanding. Five hundred dollars per month was a good salary,
and with that income you could purchase a fine family home in the
suburbs for something like $14,000.00. Glendora was beginning to
grow into a primarily residential community with the demise of the
citrus industry. The Albourne Ranch, originally over 1400 acres,
had been put up for sale in 1957 except for two and one-half acres,
including the reservoir and the packing house, which Mr. Bourne
had gifted to the Episcopal Church. He had not forgotten
Michael's pleas years earlier that the reservoir and packing house
be sold to him, and had requested that the Church give Michael the
opportunity to buy it when he was twenty years old.

Michael was still nineteen years of age when he returned
from his world travels, and the Church, finding it had no use for
the property, agreed to sell to him. Was Michael's intention at this
time to build a castle? "Not at all. I just loved to play there
because it had tunnels and elevators, and many buildings to play
in." He recalls that the Church had required a down payment of
$200.00 with the balance to be paid monthly. Dorothy was to
guarantee the loan because of Michael's age. The down payment
was made; however, he had no money for monthly payments.

The ever-resourceful Michael called Bourne in Lake Tahoe, where he was then living, complaining that, "I have no money. I can't make the payments."

Bourne was less than sympathetic, "I know."

"Why did you do this to me? You knew I had no money. What a dirty trick!"

"I know."

Michael shamelessly went on, "You've got all the money in the world and I've got none. What an awful thing to do."

"I know."

Michael acknowledges that, "I was a brat," but the good Mr. Bourne then proceeded to make the first six months' payments on Michael's behalf for the same property he had previously given to the Church. He still feels badly about the way he treated the man who had been so good to him.

The acquisition of the property was fortuitous for it gave Michael a home. He immediately moved into the packing house, which had originally been built when Bourne had a dispute with Sunkist and decided to do his own processing and packing. The packing house is one hundred and forty feet long and forty feet wide, with four large cooler compartments on one side of the main structure. These boxes have a beautiful wood finish on the interior and are insulated with a thick layer of cork. One of these cooler rooms, which are approximately ten by fifteen feet, became Michael's room. The exterior of the main structure was, and still is, of corrugated sheet metal. The roof had been removed and the discarded sheet metal was no longer on the premises. The packing house had wooden floors and wood-paneled interior walls with a small elevator to a basement which was soon to become a wine cellar. At the north end a bathroom and shower made the premises livable, but it was in very poor condition with no roof and "gookum" all over the floors.

The move into the packing house was not conventional in any respect. Michael had been advised by an attorney friend, Al Snidow, about whom we will learn more later, that the City wanted to prohibit occupation of the premises since they had been abandoned for so many years. There were no, and never had been, living accommodations and the established usage had always been of a commercial nature. Warned of the resistance he would encounter, Michael moved into the packing house at 2 a.m. in order to escape attention. In due time, the City authorities arrived and asked him what he was doing there. Michael assured them that he was a night watchman, and the authorities departed. The stage had been set for years of conflict.

It was at this time that Grandfather Deuel, then ninety-one years of age, came to California, and moved in with Michael. This marks another critical juncture in Michael's life, for Grandfather was not only a significant presence during the next ten years, but he was also a homespun philosopher, and his many common sense maxims have become an integral part of Michael's outlook on life. Typical of these adages is one of his favorites, "Don't bore people with the truth – laughter is the song of men." A book of Grandfather's sayings is one of the treasured volumes at the Castle.

Living conditions were Spartan with no electricity or gas service to the property, but then it still compared favorably to Egyptian jails. The next year was spent cleaning up the packing house and putting in a small kitchen at the north end of the building. What appeared to be the sheet metal from the original roof was located at Mead House Wrecking in Pasadena and Michael was able to buy it back for $1.00 per sheet. He was not able to pay for all of it at once and was forced to contract for the entire lot. Most of it was re-nailed in the original holes, but some did not align properly and much caulking was required to make it waterproof.

Michael was variously working in a service station and at the National Fiber and Cushioning Company, the manufacturer of paper sleeping bags, as well as a stint at a labeling service. Recall that he was also going to sea for four months during these years. Funds were still critically short, with the expenses necessary to make the packing house domestically suitable, when the six-month period ended and Bourne stopped making the payments. Again, Michael complained that, "You let me have it for six months and now they're going to take it away."

"I know," was the standard response, but this time Michael was more creative and found another source of income.

Grandfather was paying him $40.00 per month rent and Dorothy, who moved to the packing house soon after her father, was paying the same amount. A few of the other old buildings on the site were being rented for $25.00 each, per month, and occasionally Grandfather would give Michael an extra $100.00, or so, to help him with the mounting costs. The rentals, of course, were not approved dwellings and relations with the neighbors and the City were beginning to further deteriorate. There was still no residential development adjacent to the property; however, it was within a block or two away and the City's attitude was clearly to find some method to get Michael and his tenants off of the land.

This was a battle destined to go on for many years, with the determination of the City only matched by that of Michael, who had a distinct advantage by reason of his humor and resourcefulness.

A graphic example of this struggle arose over the issue of electricity. Michael had acquired an old, noisy generator to service the packing house and the tenants since the City would not allow an electrical hookup to the property. The generator would operate four or five hours a day and the tenants' premises were connected by long extension cords lying on the ground. "You could hear the crackling and sizzling when it rained," Michael laughs. The problem was exacerbated when the neighbors complained about the generator noise. Michael told Grandfather that he was going to get a couple of mufflers to put on the generator to alleviate the problem.

"Oh no, don't do that," was Grandfather's response. "I've already talked to the neighbors about starting a complaint to the City about the noise."

"Why Grandfather, that's just going to cause me more trouble and I'm in enough trouble already."

"No, Michael. They're just going to come up here and order you to turn it off because it's disturbing the peace."

"Well, what'll we do then?" Michael wanted to know.

"I'll come out with my old blue blanket over my shoulders and say, 'Now you don't want to jeopardize the health of an old man and I need my electric blanket working at night, and you know you can't jeopardize life, limb and property by turning off peoples' power.'" That's precisely what happened and the City Building Department men went away shaking their heads. The confrontation did convince the City to give Michael a small 70 amp meter hookup. Such occurrences did nothing but increase the City's frustration and determination to oust Michael.

It would be well to visualize the property at this time. The reservoir was only about half full of water and totally unsuitable for swimming. There were dead fish and rotten leaves, along with silt and algae. The grounds were surrounded by shrubbery, trees and dilapidated wire fencing. The unpaved entrance at that time was from Palm Drive, and the surrounding tracts were primarily still homes for citrus orchards. However, residential development was progressing northward on Live Oak and part of that street (across from the 2-1/2 acres) would be paved in the few years ahead. The entire area is on a hill sloping in a southerly direction and located in a potentially beautiful residential setting.

The Pharm also was the locale for a "Tree House," so named because it was constructed virtually in the lap of a giant oak tree. It was above some old garages located at ground level and was, of course, one of the illegal rentals. The "Box Factory" directly across the dirt driveway was built above more garages and a collection of antique gas pumps. These rentals were just to the south of the Packing House. There were also other old garages and outbuildings, all remarkably similar in their run down, barn-like condition. Michael always had an understanding with his tenants that they would get the cheapest rents in Glendora and they, in turn, would take care of all the small problems with the premises themselves.

Glen Speer was one of the early castle builders and a friend of Michael's from high school days. He suggested to his friend that he would like to live in the Box Factory in 1959. Michael protested that there was no water or electricity and the structure was sheet metal with no insulation or inside walls. "Well, I'd like to fix it up and live in it," Glen insisted. Dwayne Hunn, in the May, 1992, issue of the *Glendoran* observed that, "Glen's request wasn't so outlandish or foolish when stacked against all the foolish things Michael had done and still dreamed of doing. So, of course, Michael said, 'Okay.'" Hunn continues, "It wasn't long before Glen's Box Factory had electricity, running water, a drawing table, hand-made floor to ceiling bookcases made from scrap 3"x 8"'s stuffed with books and a little gas heater. Soon thereafter he had laminated and varnished old pieces of wood into stunning kitchen and bathroom sinks with flywheel knobs and wooden water flow culverts, installed recessed ceiling lighting and cut-in skylights." Glen became one of the most valuable resources in developing the Pharm and building the Castle. He excelled at creatively using the available materials, a lesson that Michael absorbed and used throughout the building process.

Most fascinating about the castle builders is the fact that they were never paid. It was a special place and time with special relationships which became a part of Michael's life and, likewise, an unforgettable experience of fun, camaraderie and dedication for all of those who participated. Michael was a modern day Pied Piper and everyone flocked to join in his projects and his dreams.

Despite the unavailability of the old swimming hole, Michael and his friends still considered the ranch as much a fun place as a workplace. Late one evening, or more correctly, early one morning around three a.m., after hours of reminiscing, planning and wine drinking, which were always favorite Pharm activities, direction for the future was settled upon and a plan hatched. They would drain the reservoir, clean it, and Michael would then raise frogs commercially in this environment. He felt there would be an excellent market for them because of the growing popularity of frogs' legs in upscale restaurants. Since it was such a grandiose plan, Skipper Landon suggested that the partying friends ambitiously begin putting it into effect immediately by draining the reservoir.

The intrepid Pharm hands located the large valve on the fourteen-inch drain pipe and managed to open it after years of non-use. This was a very large body of water when you consider the size of the reservoir, and the pressure it generated by draining downhill from the Pharm was enormous. Still, the entrepreneurs had no cause for concern until they heard police and fire sirens piercing the night air as they approached the neighborhood. Further investigation proved them wrong!

Just south of the property and down the hill some distance, developers had started a major subdivision. No homes had yet been built, but streets, curbs, gutters and sidewalks were already in place. The flow of water, mud, dead fish and slime was cutting its way through the development, tearing up streets, sidewalks and gutters. They were no match for the inordinate, unrelenting pressure of the suddenly released waters. The destruction was catastrophic. Michael told Skipper, "This is going to cost us a fortune."

The City authorities were already inquiring about the source of the destructive waters and Skipper told them it probably came from the old Dalton Dam in the hills above. In response to Michael's inquiry as to the deception, Skipper said, "It will buy us some time." Very little, as it turned out, for the City officials were soon back and the growth–minded City Manager was sure he had finally rid himself of Michael, "This will cost you the farm, Rubel!"

The Pharm hands had no reason to suspect that the drain terminated a short way down the hill from the property. But this fact did nothing to alleviate Michael's concern about his liability. Is it any surprise at this point that another resource suddenly became available to rescue the situation? Dorothy had previously suggested that her son get in touch with a local attorney she was representing in real estate transactions. Al Snidow, who later was to become a judge, had no sympathy for local government because they had denied him a lot split permit when he tried to divide his twenty acres into four 5-acre lots for his children. When he heard of Michael's plight, he offered his services without charge. After some diligent research and analysis of the property records, he found a dedicated easement existed far back in the County Records indicating that the farm was entitled to an easement through the subdivision property for the drain line.

The sub-divider, Mr. Raymond, had been equally unaware of the easement and, finding what appeared to be a useless fourteen inch pipe, had cut it out in order to facilitate the development. The developer finally accepted responsibility for the damage and actually was quite cordial to Michael when conceding his own implication in the disaster. In fact, Raymond re-connected the fifty feet of drain pipe he had removed, and the Castle drain now proceeds to the Flood control channel. What are we to conclude at this juncture? Is this just another coincidence, or is it another precursor of some magical pathway through Michael's life? You may be tempted to adopt his perception of the unseen forces which he knows operate in his world.

What was Dorothy's position with respect to the recent developments and events at the Pharm? Understand that at this time she was a member of the Glendora Planning Commission and had a responsibility to support the City's policies. Publicly, she opposed the activities at the Pharm, but she would correctly point out that it was her son's property, and what could she do to interfere with his activities? Privately, she was Michael's mother and supported him; remember, "He was just meant to live."

Dorothy also had her own agenda at the Pharm. The packing house had been restored and was becoming more of a showplace featuring oriental carpets, antiques and beautifully framed pictures from another era. The building became a natural for the parties Dorothy was introducing into this Southern California community. The activity level began accelerating at the packing house, which now was often being referred to as the "Tin Palace." The appellation was appropriate for the parties were glorious festivities, at times requiring formal attire and featuring Sally Rand and other entertainers. As previously referenced, the numbers attending often counted in the hundreds, and this was effortlessly accomplished in the large Tin Palace.

These social activities were lively and lasted long into the night on occasion, but they caused no problem for either the City or the neighbors. The reason was simple: most of those who could possibly be offended by the festivities were included as guests. Dorothy's list of friends was so all-encompassing that she could really do no wrong. The ongoing revelry was more a problem for Michael than anyone else. After all, this was his home in which the constant merrymaking and the smoke-filled, noisy galas were taking place. Fire was a constant danger that concerned him, and on at least three occasions he had put out small fires started from

45

cigarettes or other party activities. He was seeking a retreat which would provide a little more quiet and tranquility.

For the first time the reservoir became a consideration. This immense enclosure had been well cleaned after the draining calamity and Michael had made it home to hundreds of frogs. One of the added enticements for the frog business had been Papa Peck's statement to Michael that if you cut one leg off of a frog, it would grow back one in its place. Grandfather further advised Michael that Papa Peck wasn't very adept; that if the leg were skillfully cut, two would grow back in its place, thereby doubling profits. Michael didn't know any better at the time but the advice obviously made an impression, because practical joking was to become an art form at the Castle.

The venture had turned out a dismal failure; not only had not a single frog been sold for profit, but the noise generated by this many frogs croaking in discordant cadence in the dark of night was more than a minor distraction to the residents and the neighbors. The entrepreneurial spirit was not lost; it was determined the focus must be redirected, and, the frogs must go.

There was now a tunnel into the reservoir from adjacent to the entrance to the Tin Palace. This was the product of a weekend of long, arduous work by Michael, Skipper, Glen Speer and some friends of Skipper's from Vandenberg Air Force Base. Skipper was in the Air Force at this time and had brought his buddies home to Glendora on leave to enjoy a break from the military routine. The Pharm routine may have been different, but it was certainly not restful. The point should be made before continuing that the Pharm and the Castle are built on a foundation of hard work, food and fun. In fact, you will see signs at the Castle reading, "Work hard, Enjoy Life and Safety Third." The Vandenberg boys worked, along with the others, for twenty-four hours continuously to complete the tunnel, and when completed they all enjoyed a big feast, another Pharm tradition. Michael will insist that the hearty meals were not used as motivation for workers. The reason is simply, "because eating is one of the joys of life." But the feasts became a Pharm tradition which is still carried on today.

It occurred to Michael that the inside of the reservoir would be the perfect locale for his safe haven away from the Palace. Thus began the first work on a structure that would become an integral part of the Castle itself. Did he have a conventional dwelling in mind? It would probably never be the subject for a story if he had. No, Michael began building a home that was constructed from wine bottles laid horizontally and filled with concrete mortar between each bottle.

The Bottle House is quite small, about 8' by 10', with a small door. There is an upper loft, reached by vertical stairs against one wall, this being the sleeping area. The ground floor boasted a small woodstove, an old over-stuffed chair and a kerosene lamp for lighting. There were no other facilities, but he did have a five-gallon pull-chain shower outside the house and there was an outside bathroom further away on the property beyond the reservoir perimeter. The interior visual panorama created when the sun strikes the Bottle House, with its green, yellow, red and white bottles all casting their glow, is as magical as the Castle itself. It is also warm in the summer sun and very cold in the winter night. Michael fondly remembers reading by lantern light with the stove warming the cavernous concrete and glass structure. He recalls it was a most wonderful place to live. Here we must interject a note of skepticism based upon an independent account not quite in accord with his recollection.

Dwayne Hunn had returned to the Pharm in the 70's after several months' absence and, since his original dwelling, the Tree House, then had other tenants, he asked if he could remodel the old garage between the reservoir and Live Oak into a dwelling. This eventually became the Chip House, but during the process of conversion the City again began harassing Michael about the illegal activities. Michael wanted the project completed as quickly as possible in order to forestall the mounting problems. Since at this time Michael had moved back into the Tin Palace after Grandfather's death, he told Dwayne that he should live in the Bottle House until the garage conversion was completed. "Why do I have to live there?" Dwayne wanted to know. "Because I had to live in the bottle house and it inspires you to finish your project quickly," Michael responded. "When the sun comes up in the morning, it turns the place into an oven, and when the sun goes down that place just turns so cold! You can only put enough wood in the stove to last for an hour and a half. You'll get your place finished a lot quicker if you have to live in the Bottle House." Does that sound like a stirring recommendation for the aesthetic qualities of the Bottle House?

Further evidence of the limitations of the Bottle House surfaced from the events surrounding a visit Grandfather had with Michael one drizzly evening. He had brought a bottle of wine and settled in the old stuffed chair while Michael sat on an orange crate. A fire in the stove removed the edge from the chill air and Grandfather, looking around the cramped quarters, mused, "You know, Michael, you really taught me something."

"What's that, Grandfather?"

"There's more than one way to stay single."

Michael does admit that such a home tended to put a damper on any serious dating activities. Despite its limitations, there is absolutely no denying that this unique dwelling is something right from the pages of *Alice in Wonderland* and it wonderfully complements the fairy tale atmosphere of the Castle.

The projects seemed to be endless at the Pharm. They had immediately added a kitchen at the north end of the Tin Palace in order to make it livable for Grandfather, Dorothy and Michael. Glen Speer had a part time job as a stock clerk at Bock's Variety Store, an unusual occupation for someone so talented and educated, and his contributions to the ongoing development were incalculable. Dwayne Hunn, who learned most of his skills from Glenn, tells us that Michael had once said, "Glen has a gift few people have. He can look at an empty spot and visualize what could and should be there. Then he can do what even fewer people can do – he can make what should be there. When it's finished it's always beautiful. I can make things work, but they seldom look pretty working. Glen could always see it, build it, make it beautiful. And it would work. Glen is truly gifted."

There was so much activity at the Pharm with tenants, construction and visitors that parking became a problem, again bringing scrutiny by the City. The solution was to build a larger tunnel into the reservoir to allow cars to park in that area. At the same time, Michael had not given up the idea of making the property productive and began several agricultural pursuits, none of which turned out well. He tried growing cucumbers and eggplant commercially. The eggplants seemed to be perfect – they were large and beautifully colored and when Dorothy brought one of them to the kitchen and cut into it, it was almost hollow. "There was too much nitrogen in the ground, probably from over fertilizing," Michael explains. He also attempted to start a commercial vegetable garden, planting the seeds in corrugated tin troughs. The plants were protected by large sheets of plastic surrounding the bedded area. This protective shielding was destroyed by the Santa Ana winds and, again, Michael was diverted from what might have been an impediment to his real life's work – castle building.

It was about this time that Michael overheard Dorothy and Grandfather arguing, with Dorothy berating her father for encouraging Michael to engage in such seemingly frivolous projects as the frogs and agricultural follies, "He needs to go to school and learn things so he can raise a family and be a success." "Dorothy, you've got two successful kids. Let's have fun with this one," was Grandfather's portentous reply.

Grandfather was having his own fun at this time. He would always sit in the kitchen looking out the window onto Palm Drive, smoking his pipe and often drinking. He and Sally Rand were good friends even though he was about thirty years older than the entertainer. They would often start playing strip poker in the kitchen. Michael didn't mind that, but the window was only about six feet from Palm Drive and, with the curtains open and a Coleman lantern in the background to light the room, everyone going by would stop and stare at the proceedings. He was furious, "Grandfather, damn it, don't you realize I'm in enough trouble. Now people are staring in at a naked lady!"

"Oh, they all know who she is, they've seen her on TV."

"Grandpa, I can't have that sort of thing," Michael insisted.

"Oh, you're always taking the fun out of everything."

Michael inquired of Sally why she had lost all her clothes and Grandfather was still almost fully dressed, "Don't you ever win a hand?"

"I do, but he puts on studs, cufflinks and tie, and has to take off all those things first."

Grandfather seems to have taken a lesson from his mother about whom he once said, "My Mother was the wisest person. If she said it once, she said it a thousand times – 'Harry, go out and play!'" Grandfather was also hard of hearing and the impediment could be embarrassing at times because he spoke so loudly and his language was not always suitable for company. On one occasion he, Dorothy and Michael were attending the San Gabriel Symphony. During one of the classical presentations an extended pause occurred and Grandfather, thinking the concerto completed and the audience not responding with appropriate applause, blurted out, "What the f___, I thought that was pretty good." Dorothy was mortified, "Father, we just can't take you anywhere!"

The early to middle 60's witnessed the start of the gathering of materials for construction of the Castle. No one was quite sure what it was going to be, for only Michael had the plans and they were entirely in his head. But there was an eagerness to help on the part of the tenants and his many friends; people like Skipper Landon, Carl Gunn, Ed Bennett, Lorne Ward, Glen Speer, and many others, and they started gathering materials for the project. Word soon got out and whenever anyone heard of any materials available, Michael and his friends were off with the old truck to save them from the scrap pile or the dump. People dropped off bottles, bed springs, scrap metal, anything they didn't want, and the Pharm became home for them. As Dwayne Hunn has written, the neighbors failed to see the beauty in the accumulation and didn't have the vision that the Pharm hands were blessed with.

John McHann was another of the Castle builders and he began to be concerned when they needed materials and, of course, there was no money with which to purchase them *"Don't worry John, if we need something, it will be here,"* Michael reassured him. "Whatever I needed somebody always came by with one. If I needed telephone poles or a forklift or railroad ties, they would always show up. As the years went by there was a network and if I needed something or work done, the word would go out and they all would show up or bring by what was needed, or tell us where to get it. A lot of times there was too much and I had to throw it away or put it in the walls." The imagery of a castle made from leftovers begins to emerge, even to the most practical and traditional beings, and especially to the neighbors who witnessed the growing accumulation.

Michael served a six-month tour of duty with the Marine Corps Reserve during this time, and he was still going to sea with C.J. Boggs for the four-month stint each year, so the work was not continuous. The Marine Corps active duty was another strange experience for Michael. His arrival at Camp Pendleton on the day of his induction was quite unlike anything he had ever experienced. The Marine sergeants are not known for their gentleness, and the pushing and shoving he received made him wonder what had happened to the country. He had just returned from Panama, finishing a voyage with Boggs and thought maybe foreign powers had taken over. Each inductee was given a postcard and told to write home. Knowing the cards would be read, Michael addressed his card to "Pat Brown, Governor, State Capitol, Sacramento, California." The card read: "Dear Uncle Pat, I'm in the Marines now. I just got back from Panama and it looks

52

like a very interesting experience, except they use very poor language." He recalls that the Marines were always a little careful how they treated him thereafter.

"I enjoyed the whole experience," Michael says, "because I was familiar with guns and marching from my military school days and I had always used guns on the Pharm and in the mountains. But I was also bewildered because the other men always thought I was pulling the leg of the sergeant. I really wasn't; I just didn't quite see things their way. My military M.O.S. was 0731 and when I asked the sergeant what that meant, he said, 'It means you're unfit for group activity.'" Of course, Michael then wanted to know what *that* meant.

"It means when I want to know what time it is, I send you across the firing line to ask the sergeant on the other end what time it is."

"Why do you do that?" Michael wanted to know

"Because you're the first person we have to get rid of."

Meanwhile, back at the Pharm much was being done. But what was it that was being done? The Castle building could well have started without any real intent beyond the fantasy that Michael had possessed since childhood. They were gathering alluvial rocks from the fields and hills outside of town and hauling them by the truckload to the Pharm. It was brought to Michael's attention that there was as much structural steel as they wanted from a flood control project where the steel did not meet specifications. The flood control foreman would call Michael and advise that there was a stack at a certain place and, "if it's gone by tomorrow morning, it's yours." This was preferable to having to haul it away themselves, and scrap steel had very little value at that time.

Michael and friends began hauling tons of rocks from the river bed which coursed down the San Gabriel Mountains just north of Glendora. This property was controlled by the Flood Control Agency, but the Castle forces had somehow come into possession of a key to the gate. After being chased off on enough occasions, Michael happened to meet one of the County Supervisors, Frank Bonelli, at one of the many community parties. He asked if he could arrange permission for access to the river bed and removal of the rocks. Mr. Bonelli agreed to assist Michael since there was an overabundance of rock and their removal would do no harm. The next time the Flood Control employees attempted to expel the scavengers from the area, Michael showed them a letter on the Board of Supervisors stationery giving permission for the activity. Their response: "Nobody tells us anything." It was another thorn in the side of officialdom and Michael's stock took a further decline.

The acquisition of cement was another perfect example of the way things fell into Michael's lap. Building materials to this point had been cast-offs or salvaged from many sources. Remember this was all low budget stuff until into the 1980's. The seemingly insurmountable difficulty was that the Castle structure would consume thousands of tons of cement, and cement cost money that Michael did not have. When he was building the Bottle House, he had been going all the way over to Colton to shovel up the cement spills from a conveyor at a cement plant there to use for his concrete. It was hard work, but Michael loved hard work. Stanley Baird, who was a close friend and another father figure in his life, observed this laborious procedure and said, "Michael, just go down to Foothill Lumber and buy your cement and put it on my bill." Walt Wiley, at Foothill Lumber had known Michael all of his life and, when he came in and asked for fifty sacks of cement, insisted, "Give me your money first."

"No, no. Just put it on Stanley Baird's bill."

Walt was not about to believe him and said he would have to call Stanley first. When Baird told him to give Michael all the cement he wanted and just charge it to his bill, Walt was incredulous, "How did you get him to do that, he's such a tightwad?"

"He offered to do it!"

"I don't understand it. I *just* don't understand it," muttered Walt walking away.

Actually Baird was not a tightwad. He had received a sum of money when his parents sold their ranch in Porterville, and he had lent it to the McDonald brothers to help them get their hamburger stand in San Bernardino into operation. You can guess the rest; this was the start of the McDonald's chain, and the obligation was repaid when the fifteen stands which they later owned were sold to Ray Kroc. The McDonalds' had given Baird a percentage ownership in their company in lieu of the loan and his investment had multiplied exponentially.

Visualize the Castle grounds again some years after the draining of the reservoir. There are stacks of railroad ties, piles of scrap steel, railroad tracks and bottles, tons of rock, as well as the throwaways which had been dropped off at the Pharm place. All of this accumulation, the run-down rentals and the old reservoir are visible to the street and the neighborhood. At this stage of construction, or destruction, depending on your perspective, Kaia Poorbaugh visited the Pharm with a church group to see the well-known Tin Palace.

She and Michael had not met and she was in a position to render an objective opinion. After Dorothy had shown the group through the Palace, she suggested they go through the small tunnel to the reservoir to, "see the Castle." Only the bottle house and the disarray of the machine shop under construction were in evidence, but Michael helpfully pointed out where the spires and towers would one day stand. When Kaia departed and went down the hill to her home, she reported, "Those people up there are all crazy." She certainly was not thinking then of becoming the Queen of Rubelia.

So how did the Castle really start to take shape, either as an idea or a reality? Michael says somebody would ask if they could build a room here or there along the reservoir wall and he would say, "Well, if you're going to build there, we'll probably want to build something else on top, so we'll have to make it very strong. Then we'd start drinking and talking about it, and it got more exciting the drunker we got." Seriously, Michael had a vision of what the Castle would be right from the very beginning, but it was an idea that he really couldn't explain to the Pharm hands. His vision was so vivid that he could see each tower and rampart in its place, the massive entrance gate, even the large windmill which would later be mounted just outside the Castle walls.

This vision, which he really couldn't communicate to the Pharm hands, is validated by a sketch of the then non-existent Castle, which was done by Sally Rand and Sally McHann, reflecting Michael's inspiration. Later, a dragon was added to that sketch by Dick Macy and the final result is featured on the cover of this work, and even today appears on much of the correspondence emanating from Rubelia.

The question must inevitably arise how the scores of volunteer workers maintained their enthusiasm for such a nebulous goal. In those days, even Michael had absolutely no hope that work would ever be completed. "They really just worked at it because it was fun," he explains. The specter of so many people willingly laboring for so many years when nothing more than a few rows of piled rocks were in evidence, is a phenomenon that will be explored throughout this book. Hopefully, answers and then understanding will surface, providing an insight into the personality and charisma of the man who became the parent and guiding influence of the Rubel Castle.

FIVE

The Castle Rises

"Thinking stops many good things from
happening – just shut up and dig."

"It is a free country unless someone does not
like what you are doing."

Grandfather Deuel

      The urban construction process in the Sixties, as now,
involved a multitude of disciplines and procedures: site planning,
soils engineering, design, plans, specifications, structural
engineering, permits, public hearings and architectural review.
This procedure was applicable to both homes and commercial
buildings alike. We have no conception of the additional
requirements which might have been imposed for castles had they
been anticipated. This was the environment in which Michael
decided to build his Castle. Is it difficult to comprehend that he
just began building without benefit of even a single one of these
accepted methodologies? Is it believable that he never employed
the use of an instrument as elementary as a level, that there were
never printed plans of the rooms, towers, underground utilities,
never a written plan at all? Is it any surprise that the City was not
consulted nor were any permits sought? Can you understand
Grandfather saying to Michael, "This is a perfect project for you; It
has everything against it!"?

When people ask Michael, "How do you build a Castle?" his reply is as basic as was his plan, "You have to buy a shovel." The inception of construction was just that simple. The decision was made for the builders by Skipper that the structure would require very substantial footings because of the danger of earthquakes which are endemic to the area, and the weight they would have to bear. Skipper was then studying engineering at Cal Poly University and he had, as always, definite ideas about everything. Michael was used to listening to Skipper because he was so often right about so many things. Such as, who would be elected president, what the weather would be, how to move the most obstinate piece of equipment or machinery, and any other information the Pharm hands needed. Michael actually coined the saying which became a byword at Rubelia, "Skipper's always right."

Chalk lines were drawn on the floor of the reservoir where the towers, living quarters and shops would be built. The next part was the only easy aspect of the project for many years. They would have to break through the six-inch concrete floor of the reservoir to dig the ditches for the footings, which ranged from three to twelve feet in depth. The latter were necessary to support some of the larger towers and battlements. Breaking through the concrete floor was simple. Carl Gunn, another man whom Michael credits with teaching him many of the skills necessary to do what he has done, brought over a compressor and jackhammer and the floor was breached without difficulty. The next phase took more than seven years and was the motivation for one of the Pharm mottoes which was heard over and over again, "Shut up and dig."

The footings were dug entirely by hand and it was backbreaking work. There were no funds for backhoes or other power equipment, nor for hiring anyone to perform this tedious task. Doug Weakley was another Castle volunteer who provided Michael with invaluable help in digging the ditches for the footings. Michael said even though he wasn't being paid, he doesn't recall Doug ever looking for a paying job which would have been much easier. It was typical of the spirit of joining in the dream of a castle which seemed to infect everyone. Grandfather at one point could not resist asking Michael why the ditches were so deep. "Because Skipper told me to," Michael replied.

"My God, when are you going to start thinking for yourself?" Grandfather was quick to retort, but the work went on relentlessly.

The next phase of the footings involved the use of steel of any sort available as a structural component before the ditches were filled with concrete. Some structural steel was used, but also bedsprings, pipes, scrap steel which had been dropped off at the Pharm, or anything else available. The ditches were finally filled with concrete mixed the old fashioned way – in a mixer with all the ingredients being shoveled in, with the finished mixture then carried in buckets or wheelbarrows and emptied into the ditches. Michael considers fifteen hundred sacks of cement to be a conservative estimate of the amount used in this single project.

The subsurface construction was far from complete at this juncture. The reservoir floor then had to be raised a number feet to create the new Castle floor leaving an adequate underground space for drainage of the entire structure which was to be built. Remember, they were dealing with a reservoir that was essentially a self-contained tank. The drainage of wastewater and rainwater could only be accomplished if the ground level was raised, and all piping from the Castle quarters and courtyard could be installed with proper slope terminating in the large fourteen- inch drain to the Flood Control channel. A second drain also had to be installed with adequate elevation and slope to terminate in the City sewer line. These were complex problems considering that there were no plans, no survey information providing accurate elevations, and no points of reference for guidance.

The newly created subsurface space was also the locale for all plumbing, electrical conduit and gas lines to serve the *entire* Castle. Once again, reflect on the overwhelming difficulty of this phase of the construction with no plans of either the utility lines, the rooms, or of the eight thousand square foot structure itself. Everything that was being done was in Michael's head. No one else could visualize what he intended, what shape it would take or where it would be located. Most engineers would agree that what he did was really not possible in the conceptual stage, and would prove unworkable in reality. And yet it is all in place, it all worked when built, and it still functions smoothly today, almost forty years later. The underground utilities also include lines for cable TV, not then in use, because Skipper said they would be necessary in the future.

The final phase of underground construction involved filling the subsurface space with leftover concrete, junk, old steel scrap and whatever else was piling up on the property. A final fill of sand to level the floor prepared the surface for the brick courtyard that we now see. The footings were also extended upward and railroad track was set in place in the concrete as the initial element of the Castle inner walls.

It can hardly be justifiable to describe in just a few short paragraphs what was accomplished in these seven or eight years. The story can be better told by those who labored with such dedication to Michael's dream, and their thoughts will find their way into future pages. Further description could never do justice to the magnitude of the task and might result in the same dilemma Michael faced when he was once asked by a woman interviewer what it was really like to build a castle.

"You take the shovel and put it in the sand and then put it in the mixer," Michael responded, "and then you take another shovel of sand and put that in the mixer. Do that about thirty times and then you take a half sack of cement and put it in the mixer with water. And then it goes round and round and round..........."

"Now you just stop that!" the interviewer good-naturedly snapped, thinking she was being put on.

"Well, that's what it's all about. I don't know how to make it more exciting."

The earliest above-ground construction took place on the south side of the reservoir on either side of the small tunnel from the Tin Palace. Larry Stock was one of the early builders and had taken refuge at the Castle when he had nowhere else to live. The room he began building later became the Print Shop, but it originally served as his residence. He completed the first level, up to a height of about fifteen feet utilizing the format and design which Michael envisioned for the totality of the Castle itself. The rail tracks rising up from the floor were tied together with lengths of cable from the old Morris Dam to provide horizontal integrity. This network was then strengthened with structural steel interwoven into the rails and cable.

The river rock was then layered along the wall facing into the courtyard, tied together with coat hangers or other available wire, and then more hand-mixed concrete was used to mortar the rows of rock in place. The rock and mortar, although much stronger than most ordinary construction, are not necessary to the structural integrity of the walls. The rails, steel and cable comprise the inviolate skeletal framework which has allowed the Castle to stand undamaged through the most violent natural occurrences, such as the devastating Northridge Earthquake. Skipper's foresight again became invaluable for he insisted that expansion joints be built into every wall at fifty-foot intervals.

Larry Stock is an example of a phenomenon that seems common to most of the Pharm hands through the years: they have made very real successes of their lives. Larry became the owner of specialty plastics companies located in Reno, Nevada, and Mountain View, California, and also founded a business specializing in the parts and services necessary to insure the survival of the famous Pantera sports cars.

Why did Michael choose the rock and mortar façade for the Castle when it involved such strenuous work? Every stone in the Castle was lifted by hand, in fact probably lifted five times before it rested in its place in the wall. The first lift was into the truck at the river bed, then unloading from the truck on the rock pile at the Pharm, then again into the wheelbarrow to be brought into the courtyard, next into a bucket to be pulled up by block and tackle to the current building level, which could have been as high as seven stories, and finally when lifted into place on the wall. "If I hadn't been that young, I could never have done it," Michael reflects, "because when you're young you don't realize you can't do things." Certainly the overall effect of the rock façade makes the Castle the unique spectacle that it is. But the motivation may have come from early in his youth.

When he was about nine, Michael helped Papa Peck build his home in the San Gabriel Mountains. It utilized the same stone construction about halfway up the walls with a wood finish for the remainder. Michael helped with loading and carrying the rocks and just naturally began to love rocks and hard work. There is a temptation to begin thinking that everything that happened at the Castle was more an accident than anything else, but the premise becomes untenable when one considers the ultimate result.

This level of activity and the rising structure could not go unnoticed. Was the City just sitting by on the sidelines, watching the fox steal the chickens? Hardly; it is true they were now confronting a problem without precedent. Was a reservoir being repaired, or remodeled, or was there an objectionable accumulation of junk which constituted a nuisance? The City Building Department knew they didn't like what was happening, just as they didn't like the fact that tenants lived there. The problem was to identify the actual violation and take effective action; something they had not been successful in doing thus far. There was still no wall around the property and the neighbors did not appreciate the panorama before them. Harassment seemed to be the chosen approach by the City at first. There were inspectors routinely visiting to attempt to document some infraction which would be actionable.

Michael was aware of the growing opposition to his work. He also knew about another Glendora resident, an older man who lived nearby by the name of Del Wilhite. In Michael's words, Wilhite, "was the other kook in town," and he continued to build unusual, and illegal, additions to his small home. He constructed a ten-foot wall right on the sidewalk in front of his house to the frustration of the authorities. He had also built a volcano which had simulated eruptions in his living room, as well as painting very artistic and beautiful murals of the Hawaiian Islands on his home. An indoor aviary with many live birds was still another of his creative additions.

Michael was being threatened and harassed by the City and he asked Dorothy how Wilhite got away with everything he did. "Why don't you go down and ask him?" she suggested.

"How do you do this?" he asked Del. "Doesn't the City give you a bad time for building walls going straight up ten feet right from the sidewalk?"

"Oh yes," Wilhite replied helpfully. "The first thing you do is never answer a letter – never, never answer a letter. And when they come out to the house, you stick your arms straight out to the side and begin wiggling them, and bend your head way over and start screaming and shaking. They just walk away."

"That's how you get away with it?"

"Yep, they just don't know how to handle crazy people."

Michael reported the strategy to Grandfather, who suggested that he try it when the opportunity arose. And it was not long before the opportunity presented itself. A gentleman who is best referred to as "John Doe" was an inspector for the Glendora Building Department and, in Michael's words, "hated me with a passion." The passion was understandable since it was the avowed goal of the City, and Doe's particular mission, to get Michael off the property and open the way for residential development. John Doe was a constant visitor to the property pursuant to his agenda, and the next time he appeared Michael went into the whole Wilhite routine. Doe grabbed the front of Michael's shirt, furious, "Don't you *ever* pull a Del Wilhite on me!"

Further upward construction began on the other side of the tunnel from the Tin Palace, and it was here that Ed Bennett began building his own rooms with Michael's consent. Ed Bennett had begun working for Michael at age 10 when he was offered 50 cents an hour, twice what his grandfather was then paying him. The pay progressed over the years of his youth to $1.00 and then $2.00 per hour. He had worked on the early tunnels and then, "on the walls of the original pottery shop (now the Print Shop) and the Clock Tower. My project," Bennett recalls, "for the most part, was to keep the walls straight." The Clock Tower was to the North of the Print Shop and, in Ed's words, "was the largest stone wall expanse in the complex." This employment early in his youth was the beginning of a lifelong friendship and respect between Michael and Ed, who still maintains a room at the Castle and receives mail there, even though not in full-time residence.

Ed's rooms were quite large and the only condition Michael imposed on the construction was that he and the other Pharm hands would have to put on the roof. The roof was critical because they planned to build another level above Ed's quarters and it included a very large room with no inner walls. This room later became the exercise facility at the Castle, and it is fully thirty feet long by twenty feet wide. Ed's roof became the floor of the exercise room and it is ten inches thick of solid, reinforced concrete. Bring to mind again that all of this was being planned and completed with no plans or drawings. The entire complex Castle structure which we see today was completely planned, but the plans never existed anywhere but in Michael's head.

During the same period of time, the building housing the Blacksmith and Machine Shops was being constructed. This facility is separate from the Castle walls, right next to the Bottle House, and built on the south side of the courtyard. It was the genius of Glen Speer that produced this very tall, circular building using thirty five-foot long, 8" by 18" timbers as the upright columns. The columns were set three feet into the concrete base and were raised entirely by hand by Glen and Michael using a come-along assembly attached to a very tall palm tree nearby. It is incomprehensible that they could have accomplished this since even a short four or five-foot section of one of these timbers weighs almost two hundred pounds. There was no alternative, however; there were no funds to rent a crane or other power equipment.

The top five feet of the shop has alternating windows and open spaces to allow for an excellent draft for the smoke from the blacksmith fire pot. The draft effect was patterned after an Indian teepee. The vertical timbers were tied together with horizontal beams of the same size, and then the lower levels were finished with rock and mortar. The upper portion provides a beautiful contrast with a heavy wood finish.

Outside of the Castle walls, Glenn Speer was converting an old building just south of the Tin Palace into what became know as the Big Kitchen. There was so much activity going on at the Pharm, and so many meals and philosophical discussions that a locale was needed outside of the packing house. The Big Kitchen was another of Glen's creative masterpieces featuring beautiful wooden drain boards, a huge open fireplace and the Round Table (about ten feet in diameter) with chairs made out of logs and stumps. The stove came from a nearby church that was being razed. It was also where Grandfather chose to construct his still, using an acetylene water heater as no electricity or gas were available at the time.

Dorchen once attempted to light the stove, which also operated on acetylene, before she had found a match. Since the gas orifice had not been changed from its original natural gas usage, the acetylene gas accumulated rapidly. Grandfather smelled the tell-tale odor and warned her not to light it. "Oh Grandfather, You're such a fussbudget," she fired back, while doing just what he had cautioned her against. A huge explosion followed and fortunately she was not injured, but her hair was burned. Grandfather's cards were all blown off the table and Dorchen lamented, "Damn this place. Why do people have to live like this?"

The Troll's House was rising from the Castle floor beyond Ed Bennett's quarters, and it provides the first floor level below the present Castle residence now occupied by Michael and Kaia. Frank Kaiser was the initial builder on this addition, and he is one of the few Pharm hands who left in the Sixties and has not been in touch since. The Castle living quarters followed upon completion of the basic structure of the Troll's House below.

The courtyard in those days, as well as the grounds outside the reservoir, looked like some nightmarish cross-section of a building supply yard and a European city after a World War II bombing raid. There were building materials everywhere and construction progressing on many fronts. Since the building materials were, as often as not, junk and leftovers, the appearance was not aesthetically endearing to the neighbors. There were also bonfires, parties, dancing and drinking going on far into the night as the Pharm hands relaxed after their days' labors. The Castle builders were not popular in those years as was so clearly elucidated by Dwayne Hunn. The pressure was mounting on the City Building Department and they decided on a course of action.

Michael was finally served with a Red Tag Notice ordering him to stop construction. This did not seem at all justifiable to him since he had tried to get a Building Permit at one point, but had been refused; probably not unreasonably since no criteria existed for castle building in a residential neighborhood. It seemed that no alternative presented itself other than to keep building. Too much of himself and the efforts and goodwill of his many, many friends had been invested at this point to consider terminating the project and giving up the dream. The Notice was ignored.

Further Notices and threats followed, all to no avail; the work went on. The final ultimatum given by the City was that he cease construction or face criminal charges in Court. Again, he would not consider abandoning what had by then become the focus of his life. The threat of criminal action was not an idle one; charges were filed and Michael served with a Subpoena ordering him to stand trial.

There was no consideration of hiring an attorney for two reasons: he could not afford one, and he knew he had no defense. His plan was to throw himself upon the mercy of the Court, not exactly a promising prospect since then Judge Al Snidow was not assigned to the case. The proceedings were opened with the Judge asking Michael how he would plead to the charges.

"Guilty, Your Honor."

"Then you will agree to stop construction, Mr. Rubel?"

"No, Your Honor."

"If you plead guilty to building without a permit, why will you not agree to cease and desist?"

"Because I have to build my Castle, Your Honor."

"Mr. Rubel, Do you understand that I will have to put you in jail if you do not stop construction?"

"Well, Your Honor, you do what you have to do," Michael respectfully replied to the Judge, "but, I have to build a Castle."

The Judge continued the case for sentencing with a dilemma that he was quick to recognize. He was faced with the prospect of putting one of the more popular citizens of Glendora in jail for a project which had, in many ways, become a community focal point. Worse than that, Dorothy Rubel could well have been the most loved and influential person in the City, and there was hardly anyone who had not been a beneficiary of her generosity and goodwill. He was contemplating an action that could have potentially disastrous results.

The Judge decided to place the problem squarely in the lap of the City Council since it was nominally the aggrieved party in the proceeding. The Building Department was the instigator of the legal action, but the City Council was made up of citizens who had to consider re-election prospects. The Council's dilemma was exacerbated by the fact that several well-known citizens had mounted a very real threat of recalling the entire City Council if Michael were sent to jail. Their final determination was understandable: just let the matter die with no decision or sentence. The Castle project had been given implicit approval and the work continued.

Work continued on all phases of construction during the remainder of the Sixties and Pharm life never varied. Only the faces would change as some of the volunteers and tenants came and went as their lives took other paths. The community involvement, if anything, became more apparent as an increasing number of volunteers showed up for any larger project. People would just show up and ask Michael, "I hear you're building a castle. Can I help?" It seemed to have a cohesive effect on the whole town, except, of course, the close neighbors and the Building Department.

Practical joking had also surfaced as a sophisticated art form at the Pharm and Grandfather was one of the early mentors providing inspiration to the others. Michael recalls a party which Louise Lawton had given for a well-known professional photographer. Many of those who attended Dorothy's parties were on the guest list, including Frank Landon, Skipper's father, Dorothy and Michael.

Frank Landon was an amateur photographer who was extremely devoted to his hobby. He was also habitually late wherever he went, and the party was well under way before his arrival. Michael overheard Grandfather talking to the photographer and explaining that he had a friend, Frank Landon, who would be most interested in meeting and talking to him about his methods and technique.

"Would you be willing to talk to him when he arrives," Grandfather asked, "and share some of your knowledge with him?"

"Certainly," the professional volunteered, "just bring him over and introduce him."

"One thing you might remember," Grandfather said, "He is very hard of hearing and is too vain to wear a hearing aid. So you will have to speak quite loudly when you talk with him."

"That's no problem at all," the photographer added helpfully.

When Frank Landon arrived, Grandfather quickly collared him and advised that the celebrity would be happy to discuss his work with him. Frank was quite pleased and thanked Grandfather for the opportunity he had presented him.

"By the way," Grandfather added. "He's quite hard of hearing and too vain to wear a hearing aid, so you will have to speak loudly when you talk to him."

Michael still begins laughing when describing the spectacle of the two men shouting at each other while the other perplexed guests tried to politely ignore the farcical scene.

Grandfather had reached the age of 101 when he finally passed away in 1969. Michael had lost a wonderful friend and undoubtedly one of the most profoundly inspirational influences in his life. His down-to-earth philosophy, his sincere love of people and the manner in which he could bring them together and promote a feeling of goodwill and community among them, are lessons that were not lost on Michael. Few of us are blessed with the number of wonderful fathers that inhabited Michael's life, and he is the first to acknowledge how fortunate he has been.

The Sixties were only one distinct phase of the Castle story. Construction was proceeding so slowly that it was once written in the *Glendoran* Magazine that Michael was, "working on a project to construct a castle which won't be finished, even at his death." That was the perception and could well have been the ultimate reality. And although the legal battle in Court ended by default, neighborhood opposition did not dissipate. Two events then conspired to completely change the course of events at Rubelia. Before we examine them in Chapter Nine, there are other elements of this unusual story whose omission would result in a one-dimensional picture of this modern day phenomenon.

Castle compound from the air.
The Tin Palace is the long building in the lower left corner

Tunnel entrance to Castle courtyard

North side of Castle with gun tower, bell tower and San Gabriel Mountains

The reservoir before the onset of Castle construction

Top of the clock tower with top of the blacksmith shop in foreground

The intricate works of the Seth ThomasTower Clock

Raising the Clock Tower

The clock tower during construction

The Castle during construction

The Castle during construction

Michael leading Pharm Hands:
Paul Fritz, Dan Bjorklin, John McHann, Joe Asa and Walt Wiley

Some of the many antique machines and memorabilia in the
Castle courtyard

SIX

The Liberation Forces

"Good taste is the enemy of
creativity."

Grandfather Deuel

One of the staples of Pharm life during the construction
years was an early morning departure on a weekend, after a large
Castle breakfast. The objective was to liberate still another item of
inestimable value to Michael, but which had outlived its usefulness
or utility for its owner. Weekend mornings were desirable because
law enforcement activity was at a base level. The band of Castle
forces as often as not included wives, children, dogs, and
sometimes even chickens. Michael would be in his uniform of bib
front overalls and stained, floppy hat. They were not an unusually
conspicuous group to knowledgeable locals who were accustomed
to Michael's forays. But they would draw skeptical or negative
reactions from "proper folks" or the police.

The mode of travel was usually in the old Pharm jeep that
had been modified by welding a steel bed to the back end, making
it suitable for a multitude of purposes. It was often the tractor
portion of a tractor and trailer rig, or the base for a hand-operated
winch, or as a perch for one of the Castle dogs. It was not pretty; it
was functional. The trailer was even less stylish, for it was just a
set of truck wheels connected by an axle and modified with a small
cradle to secure one end of a long load, or to bear the weight of
some small piece of equipment to be transported, like a ten

74

thousand gallon steel tank. This was even more of a grass roots operation than can be imagined by the most open-minded person. Sometimes the Pharm's twenty-two year old flat bed truck or Ed Bennett's 1962 2-½ ton truck would be part of the expedition. Proper licenses and permits were usually not in evidence because Castle residents did not consider themselves subject to such punitive regulations.

It was often before sunrise when the coterie was less likely to draw much attention when departing. These trips almost always involved very hard work, but if you were to ask the participants, they would be most likely to tell you it was three parts fun to one part work. They can only be described as *events.*

One such pilgrimage was west to Azusa to bring in some lengthy telephone poles which were to serve as the tower supports for a large Castle windmill. The poles were suspended between the jeep and the trailer, but they were so long the creosoted ends were dragging on the ground and rubbing on the trailer tires. The friction created was heating the oil-based creosote to a degree that it was smoking profusely and threatening to burst into flame. The procession was only moving at about three miles per hour on the main street of Azusa.

The Azusa Police Officer who pulled alongside the jeep was not amused by the amateurish effort taking place in his jurisdiction, and told Michael to pull over.

"I can't. These poles will ignite and catch fire if I stop."

"I'm ordering you to pull over," the officer repeated, this time with more authority.

"I *can't*. You don't want the whole town to catch fire, do you?"

"You're under arrest for resisting arrest!" the Officer shouted, now furious with Michael.

Just at that moment the whole caravan was passing the Azusa city limit and moving into the town of Glendora. Michael was quick to recognize and capitalize on the obvious advantage.

"You can't arrest me. You're out of your jurisdiction!" The frustrated Officer realized his inability to act, but immediately called the Glendora Police to report the violation to the Lieutenant on duty.

"There's some guy just coming into Glendora with a jeep and dogs on it, pulling some big telephone poles and they refused to stop when I ordered them to."

"That sounds like Michael Rubel." The Glendora Police were used to such activity.

"Well, I want you to arrest him for resisting arrest."

"Oh, we can't do that," the Lieutenant responded, now getting into the spirit of things.

"Why can't you?"

"Well, he's got lots of relatives up in the hills and they've all got guns. They'll all come down shooting up the town if we arrest Michael."

"You must be kidding me?" the Officer wanted to know.

"Yes, they will. We just have to leave them alone."

Certainly one of the most memorable excursions was out to a ranch in Lompoc to disassemble and bring back a large windmill that was no longer in use. It would be a perfect addition to the Castle grounds, and it was free; and even better, it worked. This was a weekend event as the windmill was atop a steel tower sixty-five feet above ground. Entire families and their animals were all included in the crusading party.

The windmill itself was quite large, with blades twelve feet in diameter, and a motor the size of a modern auto engine. Bill Graham, a neighbor of Michael's and an officer with the U.S. Forest Service, as well as a Pharm hand, brought his family, and his pickup carrying his welding and cutting torches. All windmill blades were removed individually and lowered to the ground and the gear box was disassembled and passed to the workers waiting below. The motor case could not be removed and the decision was made, probably by Skipper, that it would have to remain on top of the tower when it was brought down.

The sixty-five foot tower and the motor case alone remained standing. "How are we going to get that thing down?" Michael asked, looking up six stories with his face portraying what Dwayne Hunn called, "that concerned look that often arose on Michael's face during his castle building years." Dwayne continues this report in the 1992 *Glendoran*:

"No problem,' said Skipper. 'Just go get me about a half dozen old mattresses.'

The next day, while the grunts ran around for mattresses and started torching and unbolting whatever Skipper told them to, Skipper wandered and pondered while looking up at the windmill. Finally, as the torcher and cutter were running out of the tower to torch and cut, Skipper said to the mattress-bearers, 'Put those there and there and there.'"

Bill Graham had cut through the two rear legs of the tower and had made partial cuts in the front two. Following Skipper's orders, ropes tied to both sides of the tower apex were attached to the trucks charged with the task of pulling the whole structure slowly down to earth. Skipper was "always right," and the plan would naturally be foolproof. But as the trucks began pulling and staying even to equalize the pull, an unseen factor came into play. The angle iron forming the tower legs had sides that were not uniform; one side was several inches wider than the other. Therefore, the forces were unequal as the tower neared the ground, moving at a pace faster than planned, and it suddenly veered. The tower hit about two or three feet to one side of the pile of mattresses, shattering the motor case. The incident caused Dwayne to coin a modified phrase, "Skipper's always right –and he's also close."

The weekend concluded with the farmer, who happened to raise pigs, sacrificing one of his better porkers for the Castle crew's celebration feast. The pieces of the motor casing were taken back to the friendly confines of Glendora and Carl Gunn, Bill Graham and Lorne Ward displayed their unique expertise. They reconstructed it, holding the pieces together with clamps and homemade jigs, and then heated the entire piece until it was almost red hot. At that point it was suitable for brazing the many pieces of casting material back into one unit. The casing then had to be slowly cooled over a three-day period in order to prevent cracking. It worked perfectly when completed and re-assembled, and the windmill still sits upon its tower of telephone poles and pumps water for Castle irrigation today.

The heavy beams used as the upright structure of the Machine Shop were also the product of Liberation Forces activity. But strategic planning was more involved in this acquisition than most. A freeway overpass under construction nearby had collapsed, causing the deaths of several people. The fatalities had resulted in litigation and the contractor had been forced into bankruptcy. He had secretly taken refuge in Mexico in order to avoid the many people and agencies who were interested in him for a multitude of potential claims. The State had closed the construction site and impounded all materials and equipment because of the litigation. The timbers were part of the impounded material and were stored on a ten-acre tract near the site.

Michael wanted those timbers and employed still another creative approach. He called one of the other contractors on the project, a Mr. Benedict, who was not involved in the lawsuits. Benedict was one of Dorothy's friends and had attended parties at the Tin Palace. When Michael told him he wanted the timbers, he advised him that everything had been impounded by the State. "I've heard that," Michael told him, "but if I could get his consent to take the beams, I could tell the State that I had his permission if they arrested me." Benedict gave Michael the contractor's sister's phone number since she was presumably the only one in contact with him. Benedict first called the sister and assured her that he had known Michael for many years and could vouch for him.

When Michael contacted the sister, she explained that Benedict had assured her that he was not hostile. "I'm sure he would love to hear from someone from here who was not after him." Michael obtained the phone number in Mexico and reached the beleaguered contractor, explaining his mission. "I just got off the phone with my sister and she explained it all to me," he told Michael. "You can have anything that's there but, of course, you have to understand that it's not mine." Michael understood, but thought it would help his cause if he had some semblance of ownership.

They agreed and the contractor suggested a further ruse. "If you're arrested, tell them you have my permission and give them my phone number here. In the meantime I'll change my phone number and they won't be able to trace me." Michael immediately contacted another of the Castle builders, John McCafferty, the owner of a large bulldozer that would be crucial to their operation. Together they loaded the beams on the large old Pharm truck and they were on their way to their new home. No one ever questioned the disappearance of the timbers, and the Bankruptcy Court had unknowingly made its contribution to the Castle.

The Clock Tower was to be built later, but the heart of this structure is a series of ten thousand gallon water tanks stacked on top of each other and bolted together. The water tanks had become available everywhere with the demise of the citrus industry and they were quickly appropriated for future use on the Pharm. The Castle forces did not have the proper equipment for hauling the tanks, which were ten feet in diameter, although they more than made up for this deficiency with inexperience and eagerness. Each tank was loaded and hauled individually after being tied with rope to the homemade two-wheel trailer and towed behind the jeep. The spectacle was one which would have been more fitting as a float in a Fourth of July Farmers Parade in a small Midwestern town. The oversized load balanced precipitously on the trailer and the jeep was performing a task which had never been asked of it in wartime years.

The Castle forces did not notice as they towed their load along Route 66, that the underpass they entered under the 210 Freeway, then under construction, was not designed with this kind of activity in mind. The tank wedged itself under the overpass and they could move it neither forward nor back. It seemed permanently in place and attempts to dislodge it only succeeded in wedging it more securely. "It was the kind of thing you could only have done in those days," Michael states. "Nowadays they'd put you in jail." The forces were used to things going wrong and they had vast experience in low cost problem-solving. The air was released from the tires and the ropes removed from the tank. There still was insufficient clearance.

The next well-reasoned step was to release the jeep from the trailer and begin ramming the trailer with it to determine if something would shake loose. It did; the huge tank not only came loose, but started rolling down the incline on which the road was built, with the Pharm hands chasing after it. It was not a dignified operation, but it was finally successfully completed and another part of the legend was in place.

Another victim of the citrus industry demise were the many old pumps used for orchard irrigation. Michael had located one and knew he had the perfect use for it at the Pharm. The first obstacle was to get the Glendora City Council to formally accept it since the owner wanted to make a donation of the ancient relic. This was successfully done with the provision that it could be located at the Pharm. The only other potential difficulties were that this particular motor and pump weighed 12 tons, was bolted down with one and one-half inch steel bolts that were completely rusted, and was located in Laverne, four miles away down Route 66. As you are by now conditioned to expect, they could not afford to rent a suitable trailer, let alone have it transported.

The problem of removing the rusted bolts was, of course, solved by Skipper Landon, whose family had dynamite and fuses from an old mining operation. He believed that shaped charges could be placed on each bolt and a single small detonation would quickly free the motor. Michael, Skipper, Klaus Schilling, Michael Keith and John McHann set out in the middle of the night to implement this plan since, although dynamite was customarily used in agricultural operations in those days, they did not want to attract undue attention. After the fuse was lit, the crew departed the scene down Route 66. Skipper looked at his watch and announced that, "It should be any time now." Just then, even from two blocks away, a huge flash lit up the sky and within minutes two police cars passed the Castle forces going toward the source of the "minor explosion." Michael was convinced they were going to jail and Klaus was berating the others because, "It's alright for you to go to jail, but I have a family and can't have this happen to me."

They escaped the scene without detection and went back the next morning to inspect their work. Not only had the bolts not budged, but every potted plant and tree located at the nursery adjacent to the site had been blown over by the concussion from the explosion. Fortunately, none of them had been damaged. The bolts were finally removed with a cutting torch, sledge hammers and chisels. The problem of transporting the giant still remained.

Michael, Skipper and friends surveyed the situation and came up with an ingenious solution. The motor was an old single cycle giant with two steel idler wheels at least six feet in diameter necessary to carry the engine's momentum after the compression stroke. "If we turn the engine over," someone suggested, "we'll be able to tow it back using the idlers as wheels." Turning over the monster required only back-breaking work and luck, both of which Michael and his loyal volunteers possessed in abundance. A humorous aspect of the tow was that each time the wheels rolled over and hit the compression stroke, the old engine belched out a deep, "uuumph," perhaps attracting more attention than the Castle forces needed at this point.

It turned out there was a further problem that had not been anticipated, despite the thorough planning which had characterized this operation. The temperature had climbed into the high 90's and the steel wheels were cutting deep grooves in the asphalt on the famous old "66." After traveling a good part of the distance home, Skipper became alarmed, "They're going to make us repave all the streets in town."

The judicious course of action was to hide out and avoid detection. They pulled the motor into a nearby orchard and managed to get it out of sight. After going back to the Castle to get sleeping bags, they slept by their treasure until about 2 a.m. the next morning. The procession could now move under safety of darkness and the asphalt had cooled sufficiently to prevent grooving. The absence of grooving was not good enough; a grayish powder from the orchard provided wheel tracks leading the rest of the way to the Pharm. The following day a Highway

Patrolman showed up and announced, "You know, we followed those grooves and white tracks all the way here, and we think it's connected to that engine right there." "Is that bad?" Michael innocently asked. "Well, no, you left some deep holes out there on Route 66, but, aaaw, forget it." The unseen spirits were still at work watching over the forces of good.

And what was the perfect use that Michael had envisioned for the 12-ton engine and pump? It operates a bird bath in the garden behind the Tin Palace, sending a small spout of water about three feet high into the air on each compression stroke, making it one of the least efficient pieces of equipment in existence.

The exhaust from this gargantuan could also have been just one more annoyance to the neighbors. But the Pharm hands solved that problem one weekend when the City had a contractor installing a sewer line adjacent to the Castle grounds on Palm Drive. The installation had progressed to a point just outside the pump house and bird bath when the weekend break occurred. The ditch had been filled covering most of the pipe already in place, but not quite. Seizing the opportunity to advance the spirit of whimsy, the Castle forces worked all weekend running the engine exhaust into the sewer line and then covering over their modification with dirt. The workers returned Monday and continued on with their installation, never suspecting that more of the pipeline had been covered.

Result? Thereafter, whenever the bird bath pump was operating, the water in neighboring toilet bowls would bubble up and manhole covers would rumble. When the neighbors found out, they loved it, and would tell people who had just moved into the area of the unusual man who lived there and the joke he had played on the City. The incident is a gentle reminder from the royalty on Live Oak and Palm Drive not to take life too seriously.

It seemed every segment of the local population had, "Castle Fever," by the end of the Sixties. School kids were no exception and scores of them became part of the Liberation Forces. Michael had taken a job as a school bus driver with the Glendora Schools in 1968 and continued in that endeavor until he retired in 1983. Most of his years were with the Azusa School District after Glendora terminated its own service. It was a job he thoroughly enjoyed and he developed a great admiration and fondness for the youths, while at the same time maintaining discipline. The position was also advantageous in several other respects. It allowed him to continue work on the Castle in the middle of the day and the late afternoon and evening. The bus was also a perfect vehicle for transportation of some of the larger items needed at the Castle. Like wine.

One morning after completing his morning route, Michael called Bill Graham and said he needed his help. Knowing that it would be an important Castle project, Bill did not even inquire what was to be done. Michael picked him up in the School Bus at his home down at the end of Palm Drive. Bill was now somewhat curious. "We're going to make a wine run," Michael informed him. They drove out to a winery and completely loaded the middle aisle of the bus up to the seat level with cases of wine for the wine cellar. Not a case was in sight as they drove back into Glendora and into the Castle gate. The unloading completed, Michael just had time to return for his afternoon run with the kids. Now the School District had made its contribution to the great Castle we see today.

How did the school kids get involved in liberation work? They may have been initially conscripted, but they later became willing volunteers. One of Michael's runs was up into the canyon above town in the location of the old Morris Dam. You will recall that the long lengths of cable for the structure were "rescued" from that site where they had previously been used as part of an abandoned military operation. While in the locale it would be wasteful not to use the aisle of the bus for some good purpose. So the kids helped him load the ¾" cable on the floor of the bus and then assisted with the unloading at the Pharm before continuing on to school. They came to just love this part of their bus ride.

Was the School District aware of what was going on? There was certainly every opportunity to find out. The first time cables were hauled, Michael's supervisor noticed that the floor of the bus was in bad condition. "How did you get the floors so scratched up?" he asked Michael. "They're a mess."

"Those kids live up in the canyon," Michael helpfully volunteered. "You know there's mud and rocks and everything up there." Thereafter, Michael and his students were careful to put cardboard on the floor in order to spare the supervisor further concern.

This is hardly a sampling of the activity which took place on the streets and highways leading in and out of Glendora for many, many years. Was there anything transported by conventional, legal means? If so, it remains to be discovered. And if discovered, it would probably be a disappointment.

SEVEN

Castle Life

"Perception is frequently more
important than the truth."

Grandfather Deuel

Life at the Castle during the construction years was
anything but conventional. It defies both the imagination and the
outsider's ability to verbalize the spirit which permeated those
times. It could only be compared to life in another place at a
different time; a life outside of our experience. The voices of those
fortunate enough to have been participants are quite revealing and
provide us with the keenest insight into a lifestyle that may never
again occur in this country. Michael was the inspiration, the
mentor and the lifeblood for the emergence of a community
consciousness unparalleled in modern times. And yet this was
accomplished in the least likely way imaginable; by providing a
vision, a dedication and a purpose and sharing it with *everyone,* but
demanding nothing of anyone. His unassuming manner, ever-
present humor and work ethic were irresistible magnetic forces.
Let's listen to those who followed.

Ed Bennett recalled those years in the July, 1999, issue of
the *Glendoran* Magazine:

"I think it was great that Michael Rubel could realize his
dream. He reminds us that we are only limited by our imagination
and he's inspired so many young people to dare to try the
Impossible. He certainly has been one of the most influential

87

persons in my life. A lot of work was accomplished through the cooperation of members of the community, both old and young. Good advice was given by seasoned builders, electricians, plumbers, etc., and the strong backs and energy needed were provided by young people. The whole project was community supported and obviously a labor of love."

The *Glendoran* article went on, "Michael Rubel always had a vast array of volunteers ready to pitch in whenever manpower demands came up. He had the ability to make hard work fun." Ed, who lived at the castle for nine years in the tree house, said that whenever the day would end, Rubel would take the workers to someplace like Carmen's for Mexican food or order pizza brought in for everyone. Every workday was special and different, and as Ed re-emphasized, "Michael made hard work respectable and fun!" One of Ed's fondest memories at the Castle was watching some baby peacocks being born and then trained by their mother "It was fascinating to see how she would urge them to leave their perch and go on to the ground. One, I remember, was just literally pushed off the landing and fell with a thud to the ground. He gathered his composure and waddled off behind the others as if nothing had happened. I thought he'd be dead or at least injured. Isn't nature wonderful? That is the thing I enjoyed so much at the Castle, the way Michael blended everything to make them all work together and co-exist in a wonderful, almost fairy tale way."

Ed also recalled the ongoing humor at Rubelia. "Another permanent fixture began as a joke. Mike's very good friend, John McCafferty, one year just before Easter decided to deliver a huge rock that was in the shape of an egg, outside the Castle gate. For years, every Easter it was wrapped in paper and painted like an Easter egg. That 'rock egg' is still there even though Michael had tried to have it removed several times unsuccessfully."

The most poetic description of Castle Lore and Life was in Dwayne Hunn's article in the March, 1992, issue of the *Glendoran* Magazine:

Every town's castle should be built by that spirit that pulls kids in to a patch of woods to slap together a tree fort. It need not be an elaborate, ornate, fancy, expensive centerpiece. It should be richly built from old ideas, recycled things scraped together and sparks of creativity nourished by sweaty work.

I think I know about this need for a castle, not because I might have been Robin Hood in a previous life, but because I lived in one in this life. Now it may be hard for today's suburbanites to relate to the need for castles or stories of its errant, childlike knights. But please try to bear with me, even if just to assure yourself that Robin I not be.

It ain't easy to build a castle in every town. The spirit it takes to build a good castle probably exists in most American communities. Whether the power structure of each American community has the sagacity to allow those spirits to build castles, determines whether castles are built. And castles built by good spirits don't all look the same. What they probably have in common more than the face of a castle with its towers, turrets, gates and moats, is freedom to pursue healthy fantasies......To ponder realities while sheltered from the increasingly regulated, bureaucratic regimented forces of the progressively civilized world outside.

Glendora ...has America's answer to the real castles of yore – a real adolescent/adult built castle. Rubel's Castle, however, is a bit more rebellious than today's tamed European castle of yore. When Harry Reasoner did his 1974 Reasoner Reports show titled, *Castles in the World,* he juxtaposed two European castles alongside his choice for America's castle - Rubelia. The European curators lamented that their castles were 'expensive' to maintain. The Head Janitor of Rubelia (ed.: Michael), however, responded, 'No, the castle was cheap to run. When I'm hungry I skin one of the Pharm chickens and pull something from the garden....Burn old wood when I'm cold. When the wind blows, windmill works. Turns the washing machine and washes our old clothes.... Nope, ain't too expensive.'

Rubelia has lots of the whimsy, irreverence and the *hard work* that turns people around or upside down. Some lose their sense or cents when stood on their head and seldom come back to drop more on the floor. Many get a kick out of being stood on their head. Some of them enjoy continually coming back for more. Some of them depart the Castle having untapped their hidden reservoir of whimsically flavored common sense. They go away with this time spent to get up from the couch back home and perform their own little

90

magic show so they too can stand the rationalists on
their heads.

Reactions? There are as many as there are people who
have visited or lived here. The intrigue of the Castle is almost
imperceptible, but it leaves its mark. No one who comes here and
absorbs some understanding of Michael and his story, ever leaves
as quite the same person. There is an almost mystical
transformation that takes place when one realizes that Michael
does believe in the existence of magic, and the materialization of
his dream seems proof enough.

A most perfect example of this phenomenon is Ted
Shepherd, another Pharm hand who lived at the Castle during the
construction years in the Sixties. Ted now lives in Annapolis,
Maryland, and responded to my request for his impressions of
Michael and Castle Life. His response is printed in its entirety, and
graphically and humorously demonstrates how the experience
affected his life. My inquiry had solicited an opinion as to the
actual identity of Michael Rubel, a question which Ted had once
raised as a part of still another hoax.

Dear Mr. Traversi,

There is no Michael Rubel. There never has been.
I can't tell whether there ever will be. I am not a
futurist. But I see no reason for there to be in a
world that strives toward progress. Do not,
however, allow something as unimportant as the
absence of the subject you are writing about to stop
you from writing about it. Imagination is the thing,
and I am impressed that you asked if your subject

existed. That showed you are prepared to move ahead with or without facts.

I first met a man who called himself Michael Rubel thirty-five or so years ago. I had a friend whose specialty was getting fired from newspaper jobs and then going on to more important newspaper jobs. He had gotten fired all the way up to the Daily News in Washington, D.C. While he was there, he met, and, I believe, dated Sally Rand. He introduced me to Sally and I took her home to Mother. Mother was entranced. She had heard about Sally Rand saving the World's Fair from audience-repelling technology. She and Sally sat and talked. After awhile, Sally fell asleep. Do not think that my mother was a poor conversationalist. She was not. Sally was tired.

I grew tired of working for National Geographic. I quit. I became a lifeguard. After that, feeling strong and self confident (I ate more than the other lifeguards; also, I saved an earring), I went West. I don't know where people in the West go when it is time to go. In the East we go west. I went to San Francisco. I was not a hippy or gay. In fact, I had never smoked dope or had a same sex experience. I hoped the San Franciscites would not think less of me for these omissions. I wanted to see the Golden Gate Bridge and Alcatraz and maybe pick up any loose nuggets that the 49-ers had lost. But, while I was there, I saw Sally Rand was there. She had seemed to like my mother, and I hadn't had anything interesting to report in my letters, so I thought I would look up Sally and then I could write to my mother and say that I had seen Sally. Not much was going on in my life, but my imagination was OK.

I started operating Sally Rand's lights. Actually, as I remember, it was one light. It had a purple thing you put over it. Sally came out wearing a body stocking and make up and so forth. She had been dancing since the world's Fair. She was tired. The purple light made her look less tired. She would dance to Chopin's Waltz in C Sharp Minor and also to something else I can't recall. When it was over and all the young men had said that their father has seen her and that they were going to tell their fathers that she was still great, then she would say, 'I hope to be seeing more of you, in which case you will be seeing more of me!' It wasn't a great closing line, not 'Remember the Maine!' or 'I shall return!' or even 'I did *not* have sex with that woman!' But people liked it.

After operating the lights for a few days or a few weeks or what have you, I said that my star lay elsewhere and I thought it probably lay around Los Angeles, as I had a hankering to become a movie star or something. Sally said she had a friend, Dorothy Rubel, who had been a Ziegfield Follies dancer, and Dorothy had a son, Michael Rubel, who had not, and I might like to meet him. Well, I thought that over, and I thought: why not? So I went to Glendora and met Dorothy and the man who said he was Michael Rubel and they said where

are you going to stay tonight and I forget what I
said, Earth or my car or a motel, who can
remember? They said you can stay in the living
room.

The living room, as you know, if you've been there
which you probably have since you can't write a
book about a guy's place unless you'd seen the
living room, was big. Actually, long. It was almost
Christmas time. There were 144 paper angels
hanging from the ceiling. I counted them. It beat
the hell out of sheep math. I didn't count the
clocks. By the ticking and tocking and the bings
and bongs and clings and clangs, I would estimate
there were between 500 and 1,000. I lay there and
twitched and tried to hold it, but I couldn't. So I
went around and tried to find a bathroom. And then,
when I did find a bathroom, I tried to remember
how it worked. The guy who said he was Michael
Rubel had told me. It went something like, 'this big
knob here, the one off the stove, don't touch that.
This lever, from an 1871 Fulton Steamship, pull
that, but not until you have primed the pump, which
is already set to go when you move that pulley over
by the sign that says Do Not Touch Live Wires –
Will Burn Off Your Reproductive Organs and Also
Any Paper Money.' I went back to bed and held it.
It was a long night.

As I recall, I stayed there a few days or a few
weeks. I didn't want to as I didn't know how long I
could hold it. But I was tired of sleeping in
campgrounds or whatever. I had hoped to find a lot

of single willing women. I had been told the West was brimming with them, but they all must have been in the bathroom or something. Anyway, Dorothy Rubel was very nice, and the man who calls himself Michael was kind of interesting. He would collect bottles. Nothing made him happier than going out and seeing lying in the street, unbroken, a nice empty, dirty bottle. He would bring them back and put them with his collection of empty bottles. It was an impressive thing to see. I believe he had cornered the market. I wanted to see what he would do with the bottles. These were days when you got two cents or five cents or something if you turned in the bottles. But he didn't turn them in. This fascinated me. I had always felt I was unchallenged when it came to doing things that had no chance of making money. But the guy who called himself Michael, wow!

From time to time, when he couldn't find empty bottles, we would buy several full bottles and drink them down. Neither of us took any great pleasure in this, but he was driven to add to his empty bottle collection, and I, wanting to show myself a man who was ready to be a friend and supporter of stupid ass causes, went along. An interesting thing happened on one of these occasions. After the third or fourth bottle, his project began to make sense. The sense didn't last. It was gone by the next morning, which is more than I can say for the headaches.

He was starting to ruin the place in those early days. There was a woman named Mrs. Friesner and she would come dust and write a low-circulation Newspaper called The Shriek. The Shriek was, I think, a money loser. It had not ads. I never saw more than one copy. You'd read it, if you could read Friesner's handwriting, and then pass it on to somebody else who had so little to do that they could spend time trying to read Friesner's handwriting. Anyway, I think the guy who calls himself Michael Rubel thought that Friesner was challenging him. To wit: Hey! I can clean your place and still have time to write a newspaper!

So, he decided to build something that was too big for her to clean. He got people from all over the place to bring in rocks. They were already bringing in bottles. It got so bad, what with the noise and the dust, that it looked like a scene from that old Depression Era movie, Grapes of Wrath, the people on their trucks in their lousy old clothes and the dust. I watched Friesner carefully to see whether she could keep up. To her credit, she did – but only for a few years. By this time there were all sorts of ugly buildings going up all over the place, also a gate, to keep people in, I think.

There was a dog named Nadia. This dog had been shot, run over, beaten up, bitten, walked on land mines, scratched, and had his paw hurt. Never once did the guy who calls himself Michael Rubel take that poor dog to the doctor. The dog didn't even have to roll over and play dead. Half the time you thought it was dead. Friesner use to come by and dust the dog now and then. I think she realized she wasn't going to keep up with the place. It was getting out of hand. The man who calls himself Michael Rubel has all sorts of alarms and peacocks and mules and a short-wave radio. The neighbors were all going to psychiatrists and al anon and church. A man named Chris used to come by. The man who said he was Michael Rubel said Chris, who was also named Rubel, was his brother. But Chris never said that. You draw your own conclusions.

I got a motorcycle. I figured I better get a motorcycle. I felt competitive. The guy who calls himself Michael Rubel had a tractor, a farm truck, Hitler's staff car, and a motorcycle. I had my choice of where I wanted to compete. I chose the motorcycle. I got one. I didn't know how it worked, but I sure enjoyed looking at it. Looking at that motorcycle beat the hell out of looking at people bringing in the rocks and bottles.

I went away. God it felt good to get away! I drove south. I saw a guy with a jackass. It was the guy who calls himself Michael Rubel. I brought him some stuff. He said he was going around the world. I thought it might be cold around the world. I think I took him a scarf. We sat in my car. One of us had gas. It wasn't me. If the gas had been lit, that guy could have gone around the world on his own jet.

I went away again. I went to Alaska, to get perspective. I came back. The place was weirder than it had been. I went to Hawaii; I thought the perspective there might be better. I came back. Same thing. I came back East. I went into therapy. I spent eleven years in therapy. I wore out three couches. The doctor said he could fix Eat A Puss complexes and High Po Con Dreea, also split personalities, serial killing tendencies, and inability to establish lasting relationships – but he finally admitted he couldn't do anything about my visions. They weren't normal visions like Jesus riding a bicycle or Napoleon on The Weakest Link. They were about a castle rising out of an orange tree with a guy pounding rocks into bottles.

Was I cured, ever? No. And that is a damned shame. Because, as a young man, and even in middle age, I think I might have contributed to society, given, as they say, something back. But I didn't. I couldn't. My DNA had been altered. I think it was the dust. However, perhaps this is my chance. I still want to leave this world a better place than it was when I found it. Not that it was all that bad then, but, you know, you want to spruce things up before they let you down.

So, here, David Traversi, is the God's honest truth. There is a California, a Glendora, even a very nice woman named Kaia. And there are bottle houses and ugly buildings and all sorts of animals, roosters, donkeys, Republicans, peacocks, even a Rotarian. And there are people who rent. These collectively make up a Neurosis called Rubelia. It is a pleasant enough malady – if you leave it at that.

David Traversi, leave it at that. When the guy who says he is Michael Rubel says he is Michael Rubel, take it with a ton of salt. Smile. Nod your head. But do not, I repeat, do NOT be taken in. Your head will turn into something that no self respecting hat would want to sit on, into something that would make the average decent neck say, 'No, I ain't going to haul *that* around!'

That is all there is to say. I expect no pity – or pay, though what I have told you is beyond any payment you could give. For I am offering you a way to stay sane. Heed my words, or, if you are not a good heeder, at least think about them.

I wish you well in your book and also in your place of residence. I have never wanted to pet a luma, but now, because of you, I think I will put that on my to do list. (After the experience with the guy who calls himself Michael Rubel, I restrict myself to a diet of soft foods and quiet activities.) Good luck and keep up the premiums on your health insurance – you will be entering dangerous territory, and mental mentoring grows more expensive by the day.

Sincerely,

Ted Shepherd

P.S. Should you run into Glen Speer or Skipper Landon, talk slowly and in a calm voice. They spent more time than I did with the guy who calls himself Michael Rubel. And I think they may have been more severely traumatized.

Scott Rubel, Michael's nephew, did not actually live at the Pharm, but he might as well have. He was there constantly and would almost always ask to stay overnight. The activity and fun at the Castle were irresistible to a young boy. He wrote at length about his uncle and the unusual and exciting life he found at Rubelia in the July, 1999, issue of the *Glendoran* Magazine. It is a treasure and must be reprinted in its entirety, for few expressions recalled from one's youth are so meaningful:

People feel sorry for me when they learn my uncle made me sleep in a refrigerator box when I was a young boy. But it wasn't bad. Okay, so the refrigerator my uncle slept in was a lot nicer than mine, but that's the way it is when you live in a citrus packing house. The grown ups get the better refrigerators. That box of mine was certainly bigger than some of my friends' bedrooms. Plus, how many kids have an airtight room that can be turned down to 28 degrees? Not many, I reckon.

In those days all four citrus refrigerators in the packing house (known then as the Tin Palace) were furnished with big old horse hair mattresses which were occupied most nights. Some people were there on short visits, others to pay rent, and some were there to help with hauling rocks and mixing the cement for what we could tell was going to be Something Big.

When you're ten years old, 'all your life' sure sounds like a long time, even if you're doing Something Big. That's how long my uncle Michael told me it would take to build the castle; all our lives. Of course, I believed him, but he was a good cook and never made me go to bed before he did, so I knew I was blessed in certain ways. There was enthusiasm and too much breakfast every day, so I stuck around. I know many *Glendoran* readers contributed their time and backs and laughter back then, and I can speak for my Uncle Michael and say he still appreciates each of you. If it weren't for all you did during the last 40 years or so, he'd still be struggling with the fourth floor. And because I'd probably be there also, wishing we could make the next story a little shorter than the last, I appreciate all your energies as well.

Of course I'm not a writer and can't think how to condense my teenage years at the castle into an article. There are certainly plenty of memories, many of which I don't have anymore. There are highlights, too. I saw my first stripper dance when I was ten years old.

Maybe that's something to talk about. I may be the youngest kid to have Sally Rand dance at his birthday party. Honestly, I don't know how it all came about, except that she was my grandmother's good friend. There she was in all her ostrich-fan glory kicking up her legs, singing happy birthday to me at the end of my first decade. Heck, she was a star, sort of like Marilyn Monroe. It made me feel like J.F.K., except she was 65 and I was ten. There I was sitting on the oriental carpet with a few friends, quiet for the first time in six years. We were all wearing masks (my birthday happens to fall on Hallowe'en) but could tell every one of us had our mouths hanging open. When Mrs. Rand finally came down off the back of that flatbed truck (ed.: the restored old 1937 truck was a fixture in the packing house), I was so traumatized that I could barely look at Lauren, the one girl I had invited over for the rest of the afternoon. Sure it was a unique experience, one most kids won't have, but I advise normal birthday parties. And another thing: don't have kids on Hallowe'en.

There weren't too many places you could be in Glendora that were as much fun as the Pharm. Everyone there had the gift of hoaxing. It may have been the atmosphere, I don't know, but there wasn't one serious person working at the place. Because of this I developed at an early age the art of keeping a straight face. You learn to do this Straight Face stuff when you never know if you're in the middle of playing a trick on someone. Those of you who wonder if conspiracies really happen: you're probably part of it. Don't crack a smile.

'Just keep a Straight Face, okay? You may give someone else away.'

Our Motto. Building Inspectors may have been the most fun to fool, right up there after Each Other and pizza delivery boys in the night. We had one inspector convinced that the whole castle was being constructed with sand and just a smidgen of cement. Michael and the rest of us were all up on the scaffolding when the inspector marched in and started digging at the mortar with his pocket knife. He sure looked confounded by something. We were keeping a Straight Face because we had already caught on that Doug Weakley, the guy on the ground operating the mixer, had the inspector going.

'Do you realize what Mixture your man out there is using?' asked the inspector.

'He's doing just what I told him to do,' replied Michael with his keen sense of never saying more than he has to.

'Are you telling me you instructed your worker to mix twenty shovels of sand with a quarter shovel of cement?' the inspector was dumbfounded, and this would have been a good time to Break Out Laughing, but we kept a Straight Face instead.

Michael replied, 'You know we're short on funds. Sand and Rocks are free, but cement is Something Else again.' Seeing as how we were on the third story of one of the towers, the inspector was looking Ashen. 'And besides, we're only going up another three or four floors, so there's nothing to worry about.'

It turns out that this inspector was on a surprise visit; the quick thinking Douglas had allowed him to look on as he shoveled sand into the spinning mixture. Then, with a demeanor that spoke of his reverence for the Dearness of Cement, Douglas scooped up a shovel-full of cement and carefully shook off first half, then another quarter of the precious powder back into the sack. After carefully whisking off a little more with his hand, he balanced the shovel and carefully weighed the portion in his mind. Taking out one more pinch with his thumb and finger and sprinkling it back into the sack, he finally threw the remainder of the scoop into the mixer and began to add water.

After watching him add water for a few seconds, the inspector asked Douglas, 'Is that all the cement you intend to put in that mixer?'

'That's all I'm Allowed to Add, sir. Instructions from Mr. Rubel.'

'But how does this structure stay afloat?'

'I just work here, sir.'

Of course this hoax is one of hundreds of thousands and, like most of them, ended with a Big Laugh all around over a pot of tea, and maybe a steak or two.

All these childhood experiences are special, of course, and I could go on and on until I can't anymore. The most precious memory is Daily Stuff

We had a routine that some people found Spartan while others took to with relish. We got up early and ate and Ate. My Uncle Michael would already be cooking Oatmeal. Boiled Cabbage, Steak, soft boiled Eggs, Toast, butter, honey from our own hives and more Oatmeal until we would hold out our plates like that orphan in the Dickens story: 'Please sir, may I stop?' This was how Michael was sure that we were all Nourished for a Day of whatever the castle asked of us. We always knew, no matter how much grunting and lifting there was, Michael would keep us giggling too. He has that gift with people, and that's what made the Castle go up.

With castle building you learn to take things One Day at a Time. That's the only way to reach the top without blueprints. Mixing concrete, picking up river rocks in the fields, irrigating the orange groves and scavenging building materials from the Old Shacks and barns as the groves gave way to housing; that was mostly honest work that kept me and a few other guys Off the Streets. I'll always have my Uncle Michael to thank for whatever Trouble I missed out on. There would always be a few afternoons a week when we could all pile into the Willy's Jeep and go up to the reservoir and Michael and we and all the dogs would take a swim and eat oranges. Skinny Dipping, we called it, quaintly. There would be nights of Huge Fires and guitars and Singing the Old songs. There would always be a fantastic dinner of Steak and boiled Cabbage and Oatmeal at the end of a long day, and man were we hungry. You could count on visits from one after another incredible Glendora Old-Timer. Michael considered each one a dad as well as a friend. They were mostly practical guys who had shaped or influenced the town in their days. They would come by to drink a pot of Tea and shake their heads and tell us we had something Wrong with us and tell racy 50-year-old jokes and donate another piece of Old Farm Equipment to the cause of the castle.

Each night I'd go back to my refrigerator box and throw my Filthy Clothes in a pile by Pancho Villa's saddle, which was being stored at the foot of my bed. Nothing would keep me awake. Not my cement-cracked hands. Not the creosote burning my arms. Not the 38 clocks ticking and chiming and cuckooing all over the packing house. Not my grandmother's Antique Doll Collection, all sitting around on the Steamer Trunks and staring at me the Live-Long Night. At times there was the sound of laughter or music, somehow left over from some party years ago. 'Hearing things,' I'd say to myself, and drift off to sleep. Not even That.

How can I end this Vignette? It's queer to feel that I grew up in the Old West. I'm only 42. I'm a Lucky Soul. People laugh at Hillary Clinton's idea that it 'takes a whole village to Raise a Kid,' but I believe her. I feel lucky to have been raised by the village that was Glendora. As a boy, I could depend on any Adult I knew. I'm lucky to have been raised by my Funny Family, watched over by Michael, and to have so many Living Heroes during my childhood: the old-timers who were there when we all needed them.

I'm lucky I had the castle to be a teenager at. Because of that, I can still giggle.

Let me tell you about kids. Kids need Heroes. Kids need belonging. Kids need work. (Okay, so, since I got asked to write this I get to have a Moral, Okay?)

Commenting on the foregoing seems to almost violate something sacred but, as usual, there is another humorous anecdote arising out of Scott's tenth birthday party. When Michael came into the room where Sally was dancing, he was horrified to see her doing her routine behind the ostrich feathers. She appeared to be naked although she was actually wearing a flesh-colored body stocking. But the kids didn't know that. Michael rushed into the kitchen where his mother was making the cake for the kids.

"Mother, do you realize Sally's taking her clothes off on the truck?"

"Well, I just told her to dance for the party," Dorothy answered, trying to calm her son.

"She doesn't even *know how* to dance!"

Michael says the kids were all there below the truck with their little mouths open, and he was seriously worried that some of the parents were going to call and complain. It was needless worry; the community was probably deeply under the spell of Rubelia by that time.

EIGHT

The Elusive Clock

"The word 'no' never built anything.
It is simply the easiest answer."

Grandfather Deuel

Among the several towers at the Castle, the planned clock tower was to be the highest and most dominant, the pinnacle of this urban fortress. Construction on the tower, which ultimately rose to a height of seventy-four feet, had begun in 1964. The work was discontinued in 1969 when a massive flood struck Glendora.

Forty-four inches of rain were recorded in a forty-two day stretch, although Dwayne Hunn recalls that something like twenty inches fell in a two-day period. The flood triggered a large and damaging mud slide which came down the San Gabriel Mountains and inundated part of the Pharm. Further delay was occasioned by the fact that Michael did not have a tower clock. This was the status of things in 1980.

He wanted a clock on the order of the Seth Thomas weight-driven, hand wound clock that was in the tower at Stanford University, and felt that one might be available somewhere in the country. He had originally seen the Stanford clock when he and Grandfather visited the campus in Northern California. Harry Deuel had graduated in the second class to matriculate from the famous University, and had been a classmate and good friend of

Herbert Hoover. The clock is such a precise instrument that it contains a mercury adjustment which compensates for changes in the length of the pendulum caused by temperature variations. Without this feature the clock would not be completely accurate at all times.

Michael's persistence is an integral part of his overall work ethic and he initiated a comprehensive search for such a mechanism. He was acquainted with the proprietor of a clock shop in Pasadena, with whom he had previously done business. Mr. Kohler did not know of any such instruments, but offered to put an ad in a trade magazine at Michael's expense, to which he had access as a dealer. Three months produced no results and Kohler did not want to be bothered further by calls, so suggested that the ad be continued with Michael's phone number. The ad specified that the desired clock was the Seth Thomas model.

Several responses were received, but none for the particular model sought. Two in particular interested Michael, but he had not yet given up on the Seth Thomas.

About a year after the ad was first run, a collect call was received at 5 a.m. from a Dr. Peabody, in Columbia, Pennsylvania, the location of one of the largest clock museums in the world. Dr. Peabody, in a slow, crusty and irritated voice asked, "Are you the one that's putting the ad in our magazine?"

"Sir, I don't know what you mean."

"You have this ad that says you want a Seth Thomas clock that runs on weights. You know that there were only six of those ever built?" continued Dr. Peabody.

"No," responded Michael, "I thought they built thousands."

"No, only six," Dr. Peabody informed Michael, "and we've been trying to get the only one that's available for sixteen years."

"You really have?"

"Yea. They won't give it to us." Peabody, who represented the Pennsylvania museum, barked back at Michael.

"Oh, I guess I have to give up on the idea," said a disappointed Michael.

"Yes," snapped Peabody, "I just told my wife that if I saw the ad one more time, I was going to call up."

It might have ended right there had not Michael fortuitously decided later to call Peabody back and ask his advice regarding the other two clocks he had been offered. He obtained Peabody's phone number from the Columbia Chamber of Commerce and called asking the secretary to talk to Dr. Peabody about a Seth Thomas clock.

"Oh my word!" The secretary excitedly blurted out, "But, he's not here right now. Are you from the Bausch and Lomb Company in New York?"

"Uh... uh." Michael stammered.

"Is this Mr. Johnson?" she asked.

"Uh," Michael again stammered, and then, wisely, hung up.

The bloodhound instinct in Michael was aroused. After getting Bausch and Lomb's New York number from Information, he placed a call and asked for Mr. Johnson.

"We have many Johnsons. Do you know his first name?" the secretary asked. When he told her he didn't, she asked what division he was in.

"It's about a tower clock," Michael struggled, with little useful information.

"We don't sell tower clocks."

Michael knew this and decided to try a different approach. He obtained a list of the several Johnsons at Bausch and Lomb in the New York area. On the second call, to an Everett Johnson, a secretary answered. Michael informed her he was calling about a Seth Thomas tower clock.

"God. You people are so dense!" the secretary fired back. "I've told you a dozen times. You do not have the money, and he does not want to talk to you!" She then hung up on Michael.

The logical deduction Michael reached was that Peabody had been repeatedly attempting to convince Bausch and Lomb to give the clock to his museum. He immediately called back and explained to the harried secretary that he had nothing to do with the other caller and that he did have money.

"You do?" she was now mollified. "They don't want to give it away."

"I know. I don't expect them to," Michael explained. He was put through to Everett Johnson and they began what turned out to be over four months of negotiations. Michael's explanation: "It was not an accident. It was a miracle."

The clock had been originally commissioned in 1890 for the Rochester, New York Tower. It was to be installed in 1895, but by that time electricity had reached the East Coast and weight driven, hand wound clocks became obsolete. It was acquired some time later by Bausch and Lomb. The Clock, still in its original crates, was placed in storage, where it had remained for eighty-five years. It turned out that the Smithsonian Institute had also wanted the clock, but it, too, had a policy of accepting gifts, but not paying for acquisitions.

The sale price was subject to the decision and approval of the Board of Directors of Bausch and Lomb, and this was not easily accomplished. There were twelve directors and Michael obtained a list of their names and addresses from his nephew in Rochester, New York, John Boles. With his usual sense of whimsy, Michael began sending all of them memorabilia from Rubel Pharms, such as tee-shirts, frisbees and balloons.

Everett Johnson, with whom Michael was in constant communication, finally told him during one telephone conversation, "All the Directors here are saying that everywhere they go, even at the country club, people are wearing Rubel tee-shirts and they are saying to me, 'When are you going to give that nut that damned clock?'" The persistence finally paid off, and one day Johnson called

Michael, who was sitting on the porch drinking tea with Lorne Ward, one of his very close friends. Ward was a very talented man who had taught Michael many of the mechanical skills necessary for his life's work, and also had donated lathes, milling machines and other equipment to the Castle machine shop. Johnson announced that the Board had arrived at a price. When he heard it, Michael was dumbfounded; it was far more than he had ever imagined. He regretfully advised Johnson that he would be unable to complete the purchase.

When he hung up, Ward asked him what the problem was. Michael related the price and his inability to pay such an enormous sum. Lorne said he would pay for the clock on condition that Michael never tell anyone the price, fearing repercussions from his family. Ward was quite wealthy and could well afford the expense, but Michael considers it one of the most generous gestures that he has ever experienced. He immediately called Everett Johnson back and almost shouted, "Sold!"

"How can you now afford it when you couldn't five minutes ago?" Johnson wanted to know.

"A friend offered to pay for it."

"I wish I had friends like that," was Everett's comeback. And this commentary bears some reflection, for it is echoed repeatedly throughout Michael's story. He is the recipient of as much generosity as he himself demonstrates to all who know him, not only in material terms, but in his willingness to give of himself.

Now arrangements had to be made for shipment of the nine crates which held the clock works. They were in Bausch and Lomb's Springfield, Massachusetts, warehouse and Michael contracted with Yellow Freight Lines for this purpose. Shipment was at Michael's expense and it was not cheap. Air mattresses had to line the truck in order to protect the delicate mechanism from damage. On the day of shipment, Yellow Lines called him and said that they had not calculated the weight of the shipment when quoting the price. He was told that one crate alone weighed thirty-four hundred pounds.

"You told us it was a damned clock, and now we're having to ship a 3400 pound crate, along with all the others," the freight man complained. Michael was bewildered and immediately called the head man at the warehouse, asking him to open the crate and see what was in it.

"I can't do that. I'll lose my job if I do," he replied, since the crates were already out of his custody and in the control of the shipper. "And if you leave it on the dock over night, it will disappear since this is not a good neighborhood."

At this point Michael was not really sure that this was the clock. The crates had never been opened and the only information regarding them had come to Everett Johnson by way of his father, who had previously worked for Bausch and Lomb. No one there had ever seen the contents of the crates. Michael hurriedly called Johnson and advised him of the problem, and that Yellow Lines wanted an additional $5000.00 for the shipping. Everett became concerned that Michael might sue him.

"No, I don't sue anybody," Michael responded, "that's not my style. But maybe if we spent all this money and got a boat anchor, we could negotiate something?"

"Oh, of course. If we misrepresent something we are selling, we would certainly make it right," Johnson assured him.

"The man who paid for it (Ward) said, 'If it's a boat anchor, maybe we can put it up on the Castle wall,'" Michael told Johnson.

"You have the neatest friends!" Johnson replied, still amazed at Michael's persistence.

The next two weeks were spent in anxious waiting by everyone involved in the Castle venture. Uncertainty was the keynote because of the prodigious weight of the large crate. When the truck did arrive a crowd quickly gathered and waited expectantly. But the driver had no forklift for the unloading since the address he was given was "Rubel Farms", and he expected that a business would have proper unloading equipment. Michael quickly went to a rental shop and obtained a forklift, almost tipping it over in his haste to get back to the Castle. When the large crate was opened and they saw it was a giant bronze bell, the driver said, "Hey, it's a bell. It says here it's a clock. What's going on?" What he had received was not only the clock works, but a pendulum and three bronze bells, which had been cast in St. Louis in 1895 and kept in storage with the clock works all those years. The chimes match anything heard in the finest cathedrals in Europe, and continue to toll the hour and half-hour for an appreciative neighborhood today.

Now somewhat dismayed because the bells had never been mentioned or considered in the negotiations, Michael called Everett Johnson and told him the heavy crate contained a bell.

"Did you want a bell?"

"Oh, yes. I'm very excited about it. Everything is here, but we haven't paid you for the bells."

"Look, Michael, if you're happy, we're happy," was Johnson's gratifying response. Michael was absolutely thrilled. "It had taken me so long to get the clock and it was more than I expected."

Michael summarizes the incredible incident: "You, know, it was such a miracle, all the little things that made it all possible – the help of Mr. Kohler, the mention of Bausch and Lomb by Dr. Peabody's secretary, the finding of Everett Johnson in a city as large as New York, the persuasion of the Board of Directors, and most of all, the help of Lorne Ward. That's what life is – all these wonderful things keep happening."

NINE

The Castle Becomes a Reality

"Change is one guarantee we
have through life."

Grandfather Deuel

We have witnessed the slow pace and labor intensive
progress that characterized the Castle during the first twelve to
sixteen years of its troubled existence. The trouble was not
endemic to the Castle builders, but rather to the building officials,
the City Manager and Council, and a few neighbors who did not
appreciate the sight of piled-up materials and some of the late-
night parties. The Pharm hands and their volunteer helpers were
busy re-creating the early days when barn raising was a cause for
community celebration. And they had the *dream* that motivated all
of them, no matter how nebulous it might seem. The hoaxing,
practical jokes, liberation crusades, Castle feasts and, yes, the hard
work were their lifeblood. They were living life as it was meant to
be lived, and the opposition was the price they were willing to pay
for doing their part to change the world.

It is useless to speculate what might have been the outcome
had nothing occurred to alter the pattern. We have been offered
statements from those who acknowledged that the Castle would
never be completed during Michael's lifetime. Michael himself
told Scott that it would take "all our lives" to complete such a
work. But Grandfather Deuel's statement that change is our one
guarantee through life was prophetic. Events did occur to change

the pattern and they were as unexpected as the rising spectacle of the Castle itself.

Summer of 1968 saw the San Gabriel Mountains ravaged with forest fires and almost stripped of vegetation. Skipper told Michael that the coming winter rains were going to cause a mudslide and destroy the Castle and the Pharm. He listened, for "Skipper was always right." Had you traveled down Palm Drive one month later, you would have been confronted with the spectacle of a large wall being constructed in the middle of that still unpaved street. It was evidence of Michael's trust in Skipper's predictions. The Pharm hands set 4" X 6" posts deep in the ground and finished the eight-foot wall with 3" X 8" planks. This activity went on during October and November and drew its share of reactions; negative and humorous. Smarter people than the Pharm folk would drive by and call out from their cars, "Hey, Noah, how's your Ark coming?" When early winter had seen virtually no rain, even a slight mist would prompt the townspeople to ask Michael, "Is this the flood, Michael?"

The locals were also inconvenienced by the wall, for Palm Drive became a one-way street and traffic would have to wait at one end of the wall while an oncoming vehicle passed in the other direction. Complaints to the City produced no resolution, for Michael, unused to following directives from that body, responded that it was his right to do just what he was doing to protect his property.

The City finally took the dispute to Judge Al Snidow. He found that Michael's deed gave him ownership to the middle of the street. Since Palm Drive was not a dedicated city street at that time, Michael was found to be perfectly within his rights. Popularity was not a desired goal in Michael's scheme of things, but neither was he insensitive to complaints from neighbors. In fact, one of his first considerations during all construction was how it would impact the neighbors.

Michael began to become very concerned about the ongoing complaints and ill will created by the wall in January, 1969, when the area had only received a few inches of rain. "What if we don't get a flood?" Michael asked Skipper. "Everybody is very angry at me and thinks I'm a nut." Skipper suggested that he wait two more months and then remove the wall if his prediction had not materialized. This was little consolation to the Castle Janitor, who by then was *very* sensitive to the complaints and ridicule being directed at him.

In late January, the torrential rains came and gave no indication of ever stopping. The devastation was so widespread that *National Geographic* featured the Pharm in its October, 1969 centerfold, and pictures of the Pharm hands working to stem the flow of mud and save the neighborhood were a prominent part of the coverage. Michael, Glen, Skipper and Dwayne appear in one photo, donned in full rain gear, working to avert a breach in the wall. Near them was a sign fashioned by the Pharm hands reading, "All Mud Turn Left." The slide destroyed many homes as a wall of mud, eight-feet high, moved down the mountain inundating or destroying everything in its path. The wall was breached in places but Michael's crew, working day and night, were replacing it with sand bags which they had gathered from many neighboring communities.

The Pharm hands became the most valuable community resource in the battle against the relentless mud. They were assisted by volunteers from many quarters. Dwayne was teaching at a local high school at the time and all of his students appeared at the Pharm for days on end to assist the regulars. Inmates of a juvenile correctional institution and members of the military from a nearby U.S. Navy base came to lend a hand to the Castle forces. There were, at times, more than a hundred Pharm volunteers and Michael was sending large groups of them out to assist the neighbors whose homes were in jeopardy. He was singularly given credit for saving much of the neighborhood, and from that moment in time has always been revered by his neighbors.

The Flood Control Authority had set up headquarters nearby, but Michael reports they were accomplishing little to rectify the moving wall of mud. Skipper felt it was time to take things into his own hands. He commandeered a large Caterpillar bulldozer that was sitting idle next to the Flood Control headquarters. He operated the machine for endless hours, moving the mud to one side of the wall or the other in order to divert the flow and minimize damage to all the homes in the area.

The Flood Control people were furious and demanded that he return the bulldozer. Skipper refused, reasoning that they were not utilizing it to alleviate the growing damage. Skipper's refusal resulted in the Flood Control calling the Police and Highway Patrol. A Patrol Officer was first on the scene and ordered Skipper off the large equipment. Again, he refused as the situation was so volatile and demanded immediate action.

The Officer pulled his gun on Skipper and once more ordered him off, the confrontation then becoming more volatile than the storm. "You'd better get to your car or you're going to lose it," Skipper pointed out to the Highway Patrol Officer, noticing that the Patrol vehicle was being carried away by the moving wall of mud. The Officer lost all interest in Skipper and the bulldozer and left to rescue his car. Skipper operated the equipment until it ran out of fuel and was instrumental, along with all of the Pharm hands' efforts, in averting substantially more damage than actually occurred.

The Flood Control people came to Michael after the earth movement had stabilized and demanded to know who was operating the bulldozer. Claiming that running the equipment out of fuel had damaged the injectors and caused substantial other damage, they intended to press charges. Michael was not any help to them in establishing the identity of the perpetrator and the situation was forgotten, perhaps to not call any further attention to the Flood Control Authority's inaction during the crisis.

Part of Michael's wall had been breached during the slide and there was a major encroachment of mud on the eastern edge of the property. It found a path through the packing house and destroyed the kitchen on the north end. Many days were spent cleaning the resulting damage to the Tin Palace, but then Michael's emphasis was shifted to the potential damage which the mud could cause in the basement. Dry rot and termites were always a concern of his because of the wood construction, and he asked Dwayne one day if he could help him. Assured that they would be done in time for Dwayne to get to a meeting he had to attend at his school, they went down the elevator to investigate and determine if they could rescue some of the Pharm's more valuable resources. There was a small anteroom outside the big wooden-latch door which led to the wine cellar. When it was opened they were hit with a wall of mud which oozed out and filled both rooms to a depth of several feet.

Some of the one-gallon bottles of Sauterne, the Pharm's favorite, were sluiced out with the mud and they were attempting to save these while also pushing the mud out with their hands.

They were actually swimming in the mud in order to do these tasks.

"Be careful," Michael cautioned Dwayne.

"What do you mean?"

"Well just be careful. If you feel anything moving around, don't move."

"What are you talking about?" Dwayne was beginning to get concerned.

"Well, you know, if you feel something slimy slithering around….."

"You mean……" Dwayne was then very concerned.

"Yeah, you know, all those snakes that were up in the mountains, they might have washed down in the flood."

Dwayne let out a yell, wanting to get out with no further delay.

"Just be calm," Michael assured him, "if you get bitten we'll still be alright. I can get you out." The practical joking at the Castle had only been very briefly suspended during the worst of the storm.

An unexpected by-product of the storm and mudslide was the overnight transition of the Castle forces from neighborhood nuisances to hometown heroes. Everyone in the area realized how crucial they had been in saving much of the neighborhood, and it put an almost immediate end to the complaints that had plagued them previously. Strangely enough, Michael and his Castle have been considered as one of the most valuable community resources ever since that devastating winter. The City Council was sensitive to this shift in public opinion and realized their opposition was no longer finding any community support. The City finally capitulated and gave the Castle a 600 amp electrical service, a factor making further development much more feasible.

Was the lesson of the flood and mudslide lost on Michael and the Pharm hands? The very existence of Rubelia had been threatened by natural forces far more effective than those ever marshaled by the City of Glendora. Michael determined that his life's work would not be left vulnerable again, and construction soon began on the eight-foot cinder block wall that now surrounds the property. It was strengthened with structural steel and mortared with concrete. Not only would it serve as a bulwark against any such future catastrophe, but it would also insulate the neighborhood from the ongoing construction activity and the accumulation of building materials and assorted treasures dear to Michael's heart. It was inevitable that the wall would provoke further City objections. The City was concerned that the Pharm hands would build the wall, and more bottles and other discarded junk would find their way into the construction. They consented to the wall as planned, but required that it be built by a licensed contractor.

The wall was first erected along Live Oak Avenue, which was then the side of the compound, the entrance still being on Palm Drive. There was no restriction against building a wall that size right up to the sidewalk on the side of a corner property, but a front wall required a set-back. This would not be possible on Palm Drive because of the proximity of the north Castle wall to the future sidewalk location. We are used to seeing Michael come up with an ingenious solution and this was no exception. When the wall was completed along Palm Drive, he changed the address of the Castle to Live Oak and opened a new entrance on that street. He was found to legally have the right to change his address, and the entire wall now stands with no setback.

Change also came in an entirely different format than the natural devastation of the flood. Michael received a very official looking letter in 1969 from the Bank of Zurich in Switzerland, advising him that he had been designated as a beneficiary in the Will of C. J. Schmidt, otherwise known as C.J. Boggs. It instructed him to appear at the Bank at the date and time of the Will reading to identify himself and perfect his claim. Michael could hardly pay for utilities, let alone travel to Switzerland. He also became suspicious that the letter was a practical joke initiated by Skipper, "You've got to tell me the truth. This will ruin me if I go there and you've just been playing a joke on me." Skipper reassured him that he had nothing to do with it, but there was still some uncertainty since he didn't really believe that Boggs had liked him.

The next step was to call the Bank and ask if this verification could be accomplished by phone or letter. Bank officials advised him that there could be no exception to their rules, and furthermore, they were not authorized to inform him of the size or nature of the bequest. The only recourse was to attempt to borrow the money to finance the trip. He approached Victor Hodges, then the Manager of the local Bank of America, with this somewhat unusual request:

"I want to borrow $1700.00, and then I'm going to quit my job and leave the country," Michael told the skeptical Hodges.

"How are you planning to repay the loan?" Hodges wanted to know.

"I've been notified that I have an inheritance in Switzerland, and I'll use that to pay it back." The Manager gave him the loan only "because it was the most outlandish story I've ever been told." Mr. Hodges actually related the story at his retirement dinner which Michael attended with Dorothy.

He arrived in Zurich two days before the Will reading and had no money to pay for a hotel. Asking the banker who had contacted him if he could provide the necessary verification early and then return home resulted in still another refusal to depart from Bank rules. Frustrated and broke, Michael took up residence under a bridge across the street from the bank. The amenities were probably quite similar to those of the Bottle House and worked no real hardship on Michael. But it did provoke a bit of humor on the day of the reading when Michael was asked for his local address. "I'm staying under that bridge over there," he said, pointing across the street.

The inheritance proved to be quite substantial, in fact, more than Boggs had left his adopted daughter. Michael tried to disclaim, being severely embarrassed at this perceived inequity. She wouldn't hear of it, telling him that her father had cared a great deal about him, and besides, she and her husband were quite wealthy in their own right. When queried why her father was so generous to him, she could only explain that Boggs thought "he was funny." The inheritance was a, "Godsend. I would never have been able to do what I wanted to do, to build this castle, without that inheritance."

It was almost a year before the bulk of the funds from the inheritance were actually received, and, in the meantime, construction proceeded as before with the completion of the living quarters and many of the Castle shops. With the acquisition of the historic Seth Thomas timepiece, work began in earnest on the clock tower. The ten thousand gallon tanks had been transported to the Pharm with little more incident than getting stuck under a freeway overpass. But converting them into the framework for a tower was anything but a simple task. Lying on the ground inside the Castle yard, one was bolted to another and then to still another. The process was repeated until the full height of the tower was resting horizontally in the courtyard. Fearing that the raising process might crumple some of the tanks, they attached telephone poles as splints on either side. Raising the sixty-five foot long monstrosity now became the challenge

Resourceful and well-financed builders would have used a crane to lift the tower, but the Pharm hands were possessed of only the former attribute. The lifting operation was again directed by Skipper, with crews on both sides of the wall using walkie-talkies for instant coordination. Skipper was wearing a white shirt as was his habit, making it imperative that he not engage in physical labor. The Edison Electric Company was somehow persuaded to attach a pulley to the top of one of the one hundred-foot tall palm trees outside the Castle wall, near the tower site, and a ¼" cable was threaded through it after being tied around the tank.

The cable was to be pulled by a truck and two tractors placed outside the wall on Palm Drive. The truck was loaded with rocks because they feared the tower weight would be too much for the pulling vehicles; and it was. The truck was lifted off the ground with the first pull and threatened to roll over. "Stop! Stop!" Skipper yelled into the Walkie-talkie. Directions were shouted over the radios to slow down the well-planned operation. Fortunately, the truck settled and the tower began its climb into the sky. But once near an upright position it started to fall in the other direction. We can never be sure how it managed to settle into the upright position, but Larry, Curley and Moe had once again triumphed. The sixty-five foot section then had to be lifted atop a ten-foot tank which was already in place, a feat accomplished by a combination of people lifting with 4" x 4"s under the tower and a further pull on the cable.

Some enterprising Pharm hand had painted "U.S.A." and "Apollo 13" on the tower before the rock and concrete facing had been applied, since the general shape, with a smaller tank on the top of the structure, lent itself to such imaginative whimsy. Sure enough, the unpredictability of the Castle builders did generate some neighborhood reaction to this spectacle. A woman who lived within sight of the Castle appeared one day and approached Michael.

"My husband says you're building a rocket."

"Yes," Michael replied, never one to say more than necessary.

"Is that it?" she inquired, looking at the Apollo 13.

"Yes."

"My husband says if you set it off, you'll blow up the whole neighborhood."

"That's what I've been told by some other people, too."

The woman was furious, left and called the police and the Mayor, the latter telling her not to worry about it because Michael, "is always pulling pranks." This was apparently not satisfactory because her husband appeared soon after and said, "Michael, I want you to come with me right now and tell my wife you're joking and not going to set it off." Realizing that his humor was not being appreciated, he reassured her and apologized for her discomfiture. But even today, Michael speaks with obvious satisfaction about the success of the ruse.

The inheritance funds arrived at a most opportune time. Far more serious than the slow pace of construction, was the fact that Michael was breaking down physically. The many years of arduous work and strenuous lifting had taken their toll on his back. The pain had become almost intolerable and he was relying on others to coordinate and manage the ongoing construction. Two Pharm hands stand out in particular and Michael acknowledges that the Castle never would have been completed without them: Curt Billings and Ed Bennett.

Curt was a student in one of Ron Riegel's classes, Ron being another Pharm tenant and one of the principal motivators for the builders. Ron had taught Curt technical drawing and recommended that he seek work at the Castle while only 14 years of age. Curt was a very willing and energetic worker, his first job helping to build the graveyard that inhabits the southern edge of the Pharm. He was paid $1.00 per hour for that work and then asked if he could come back and work for free thereafter. Of course, Michael accepted the offer because he was such a valuable asset. When Michael's body became too consumed with pain and his spirits were sagging with discouragement, it was Curt who took over and kept the project moving forward. The inheritance funds allowed Michael to begin paying Curt again, for now he had become essential to the ongoing work. Curt had learned quickly and assimilated the technique and skills that were employed in Castle building. Curt also taught himself to do tile work, and laid all of the Italian ceramic tile which graces the floors of most of the Castle residence and shops.

Boggs' legacy also provided Michael with the means to accelerate the construction process. Twenty years had been devoted to the construction of the southern half of the Castle. The north side was finished in eight years by contracting for the hauling of rocks and ordering ready-mix concrete. Scott was then operating a concrete pumping business and Michael would call him when they were ready for a pour. Scott would make the arrangements with the concrete company and the ready-mix was poured on the assigned day for a large section of wall in which the rocks had been placed, rather than layer by layer as in the past. This was a luxury that the Castle forces had never enjoyed when the lack of funds had dictated the work methodology.

The pain finally became too much for Michael to bear and he reluctantly went to a doctor. It was determined that he had suffered severe disc damage between several vertebrae and would require surgery. The surgery was not entirely successful and he was left with crippling pain, requiring confinement to a wheelchair for four months. Even when out of the wheelchair, he was in constant debilitating pain for the next four years. Again, Michael credits a miracle for the continuance of the Castle project after his hospitalization, for by then Curt had moved on to a regular job. The first day Michael appeared at the Castle in his wheelchair after discharge, Ed Bennett returned from a stint of gold mining and immediately took charge of the work at that juncture. He was also intimately familiar with the construction methods and willingly lent his skills to the completion of this work of destiny.

It would be a mistake to conclude that the Building Department harassment had subsided just because the City Council and the neighbors were now members of the pro-Castle cause. The new entrance on Live Oak was guarded by a massive wooden gate constructed primarily by Bill Graham. Michael provided the hydraulic opener and the electronic controls, permitting operation on site or remotely from the Castle residence. A pedestrian entrance is immediately adjacent with similar electronic controls and a doorbell that rings in the Castle.

Skipper had conceived of a fine practical joke, hoping to catch Michael, or another Pharm hand, by surprise. He had wired an old Ford coil to the doorbell button at the pedestrian gate. Unfortunately, the next person to use the doorbell was John Doe, the dedicated Building Inspector who had given so much grief to the Pharm hands.

"I'm going to have you arrested for attempted murder," he shouted upon entry to a completely bewildered Michael, who asked why.

"You tried to electrocute me!"

"How did I do that?"

"You know very well how you did it. You can't go around electrocuting people!" Doe again shouted.

"Well, if I did, it didn't work did it?" It goes without saying that Mr. Doe did not appreciate Michael's sense of humor.

The post-flood era also saw the first appearance of George Campbell at the Pharm. If you were walking up Live Oak after the cinder block wall had been built, you might have seen a somewhat nondescript man in old, dirty clothes weeding or working near the street. If you were curious about what was going on behind those walls with towers rising above the trees, and asked him if you could go in and see that place, you would have heard something like this:

"Well, I'm George Campbell and I'm the gardener here. I can't let you in."

If you happened to phone the Castle in those years and ask to talk to Michael, you might have gotten this response:

"I'm George, and he's down in the tunnel with Crazy Bill, and he's kind of mad at me, so I don't dare go down there."

If you asked him to have Michael call, he would probably respond, "I guess," but when you asked him to write your number down you were certain to hear:

"Well, I don't know how to write."

If you were to later call and get Michael, you might have suggested that he get a new gardener because George seemed like an absolute idiot.

"Oh, I know he is," Michael would answer. "He can't read or write and he's just so stupid."

If you were to then suggest that George sounded an awful lot like Michael, he would have said:

"I know. He's imitating my voice all the time."

Michael loved this "other self", and used the persona to avoid undue disturbances during the busy construction years. The ruse no longer worked after Michael and the Castle were featured on a segment of Huell Howser's television program, *California's Gold*. Everyone recognized him after that and George went into early retirement. Crazy Bill was another creation of the Pharm hands to discourage people, mainly kids, from wandering down into the open tunnels on the property. Michael would find large rocks that had fallen in these tunnels, and did everything possible to make the subterranean passages mysterious and unfriendly, hoping to avoid serious accidents.

Castle construction was finally nearing completion in the Eighties with the infusion of money from the C.J. Boggs beneficence. But to emulate the Castle compounds of the Middle Ages, one more feature was required for authenticity: a cemetery. Since Michael is both respectful and irreverent, a strange but workable amalgamation, this would be the perfect irony for the years of animated existence everyone had experienced there. You will find marble headstones inscribed with the names of many still-living friends, some with boots protruding out of the burial plot.

There are also memorial stones for many he has cared deeply about, such as Odo Stade, Sedley "Papa" Peck and Heinz and Dorothy Rubel. Many of the stones were rejects from a local monument manufacturer. There are those which commemorate significant events like the flood, and those containing verses similar to the ones found in the old cemeteries of the early west, such as, "He loved us. We loved him. Bill Brown 1927 – 1974," "Be good S.E.D. 1862," "Maud Aunte Baxter Dec, 22, 1873 – Aug. 1, 1973, 'I told them I was sick'" and "To Tasha – Best Woofie in the world. November 1989." Strangely enough, the site *was* an actual burial ground when the property was owned by the Rubidoux family in the 1860's.

The years of work gave way to a realization that there are no obstacles which can not be overcome; that the determination to realize a dream is a vital part of the dream, and that the materialization of the dream should not be surprising if we have an innate understanding of the reality of our existence. Michael has always intuitively possessed these realizations. And the Castle, once completed, took its place among the other "works of art" in the world, and it is home to the King and Queen of Rubelia.

Santa Fe caboose and other residents

One of the cemetery headstones

Dr. Henry A. Kissinger

November 1, 1987

Dearest Flo,

We all enjoyed seeing you again. Let us
return your hospitality when you visit Washington.

I was with the Duke of Edinburgh recently
in Colorado. We discvoered we had something
in common in our visits to your friend's
castle.

My warmest regards to you,

Henry

HAK:is

Kissinger letter to Flo Flo Peck about Castle

Celebration of Castle completion at Rubelia on May 4, 1986

Celebrants on Glendora Street find restaurant closed

Castle completion celebrants enroute to restaurant

Romeos: Warren Asa, Warren Bowen, Michael and Dick Macy

Michael in a reflective moment

TEN

The Pharm Hands

"Delete your need to understand –
things are as they are."

Grandfather Deuel

What would possess a large number of people to devote a significant period of their lives to a cause so abstruse as to almost be an enigma? What could possibly be so compelling as to motivate such a group to want to haul rocks, or gather scrap iron, or hand-mix concrete for a "castle" which they certainly could not visualize, and which would not be finished for twenty or thirty years? Were they being rewarded for their efforts to a degree that eliminated the need for it to make sense? The answers to these questions are the real story of Rubelia. For there is a deeper meaning here that far exceeds the material accomplishments.

Rubelia and its Castle is a national treasure, being one of the most unique and innovative edifices of our time. As incredible as Michael's creation might seem, it was only a catalyst for a phenomenon that is a rarity in these days of high-speed civilization. The Castle represents a spirit weaving its way through the life of every person who joined in this "impossible venture." Not a single soul at Rubel Pharms questioned the value of what they were doing or the importance of their efforts. They *believed*; they worked without doubt or uncertainty; they loved each other and the nobility of their cause; they laughed and muddled together;

135

and most importantly, they were living life as they knew it was meant to be lived.

We understand that every pursuit requires a purpose in order to be meaningful. If the purpose is unknown, or seems beyond reach, then the pursuit becomes spiritual in nature, and its meaning is found in the inner recesses of our being. Each participant in Michael's world would be most likely to tell you it was one of the most important periods in their life. And yet, they could not have even imagined what he had in mind. They must have sensed that he intuitively understood the spirit which bonds men and the forces which operate in the universe. How else can we explain the events that are chronicled here?

The person who became a Pharm hand brought something both singular and exceptional to the amalgam that became Rubelia. We can only speculate what there was about Michael or the Pharm that made it seem a desirable place to be, but it is certain that if a team were being consciously assembled, the composition would have been much the same. There were far more than the few mentioned in this work, and their contributions were of no less importance or worthy of note. It should be obvious by now that no one was there for the notoriety it brought. A look at a few of the "hands" will give the reader some notion of why Michael holds all of them in such high regard.

GLEN SPEER. One of the most talented and creative men Michael has ever known, yet quiet and almost shy. When he first arrived at the Pharm, he worked part-time at Bock's Variety Store, having become disillusioned at architectural school. The list of his contributions to the Castle is most impressive: the beautifully restored Box Factory where he lived, The Big Kitchen with its Round Table, the massive and distinctive center structure of the

Machine and Blacksmith Shop, the beautifully restored 1927 Chevrolet delivery truck which is now the centerpiece in the Tin Palace, the Pharm swimming/fish pool fashioned from one of the ten thousand gallon tanks and, finally, the Tree House, with its spacious deck and curving staircase, a project which Glen designed and built with Dwayne Hunn.

Dwayne remembers that he wanted to remodel the Tree House when he moved in, but Michael would not let him do anything without Glen's OK. When asked, Glen suggested they start right in and, grabbing a sledge hammer, began demolishing a wall. Michael, hearing the devastation taking place, came up the stairs and saw the wall already knocked out. He immediately paled. "Oh, my God!" was all he could say before returning to his room in the packing house to drink wine. Michael later told Glen he thought it had been a bearing wall, but Glen hadn't thought so, although he was not really sure. The restoration was beautiful, a typical Speer creation.

One day Glen went to the library and returned with a stack of educational books which turned out to be on framing windows.

"But, Glen, you know how to frame windows," Michael and Dwayne were quick to remind him.

"Oh no," Glen responded, "framing windows and doors is a lot more complicated than you realize. I figured I had better understand how it is done."

Dwayne remembers that he and Michael looked at each other in disbelief that someone as talented as Glen would study many more books about a skill at which he was already most adept. "He was a student of everything," Dwayne recalls. "He had decided that he had to go out and make it in the real world, outside the Pharm."

Glen had accepted a job as a window framer for a construction company in the U.S. Virgin Islands. The Pharm hands all thought he would be running the company before long, and that's actually what happened. Dwayne traced his progress in the May, 1992 issue of the *Glendoran*: "It wasn't very long before he moved from window framer to foreman. It was during that job progression, which in Glen's work ethic made his work day 16 hours long and usually seven days a week that he realized, although he never said it, that he knew more about building than anyone else on the island. So Glen, along with a hip partner, possessed of much more casual work ethic who lived in the middle of the island in a large well-stocked tent, formed their own company, Lollop Construction."

Glen, who went through two different partners, built the most beautiful homes on St. John Island and paid the best wages to his mostly native crew, but ended up with little himself. Dwayne reported that, "His rich clients always seemed to nickel and dime him," and after a few years, "he had lots of equipment, beautifully done projects, many more headaches, but little money in the bank." He missed his friends and the Pharm and had decided it was time to sell out and go back with the people he liked.

When he was preparing to leave, the retired Chairman of the Board of Dow Chemical Corning Ware, whose home Glen had built, introduced him to the new Chairman, who also wanted a home built. Citing his disappointment with past clients, who were always making late changes, and bickering over amounts charged, Glen explained that he was quitting business. The Chairman offered to pay Glen for the money he had lost as well as paying

138

him in advance for the home he wanted built. "Just tell me when and for how much you want the next checks and I will send them." Dwayne reports that he told Glen, "Design and build me a house something like this one and tell me when it is done. That's all I'll ask of you."

That was the beginning of Glen's extremely successful career in the Virgin Islands, which culminated in the construction of the stunning Mongoose Junction shopping mall, created out of fine Caribbean woods and native stones. Glen did return to the Castle in 1986 for his wedding, a celebration attended by many of the Pharm hands. Dwayne Hunn, with his intuitive perception of the Castle spirit, hailed Glen as the guy who, "...personified the work ethic, insight, knowledge and vision that those of us growing at the castle were trying to take into the real world."

CURT BILLINGS. Michael was always very concerned that someone might be hurt during the building of the Castle, particularly because of the makeshift approach usually employed. Curt was definitely one of Michael's favorites, beginning as a boy and working on into manhood, due to his eagerness and willingness to learn. The usual response to everything he was told was, "Yes, Mr. Rubel," or "Right away, Mr. Rubel." When the clock tower was being raised and the entire colossus threatened to fall, Michael took Curt aside and cautioned him.

"Curt, you have to be very careful because my life is in your hands."

"Yes sir," Curt replied.

"No, I mean it," Michael told him. "I'm really serious."

"Yes sir."

"Curt, do you know what I mean?" Michael persisted.

"Well.........," was all Curt could think of.

"Curt, let me tell you. I love you very much," Michael explained, "and if you should fall and hurt yourself seriously, I'll kill myself. So my life is really in your hands. If something happens to you, my life is done."

Among the Pharm buildings outside the Castle walls is an attractive horse stable and corral constructed of the same rock and concrete design as the rest of the Castle. Above the stable door is a sign reading, "Billings Barn." When he was about twenty years of age, Curt announced that he wanted to build one Castle building entirely on his own, and this was his personal endowment for the legacy of Rubelia.

Michael's concern for Curt was so genuine that he finally forced him to leave his work at the Castle, and go out into the world to pursue a career which would serve him well in the future. Curt was worried that he had done something wrong, but he was assured that such was not the case. He initially applied at Kim Lighting and explained that he had worked for Michael for eight years. When Kim inquired of Michael, he told him that he could not hire a nicer, more honest or hardworking person in the whole world.

Curt worked there for three years and then took a position with the Rancho Cucamonga Engineering Department, despite the fact that he had no formal education beyond high school. His training in Ron Riegel's class as a draftsman and his experience at the Castle, along with a recommendation from Michael, won him the position. His skills and personality are so outstanding that he is now the Assistant City Engineer. Another of the Castle success stories.

FRANK "SKIPPER" LANDON. Skipper was an integral part of Michael's life from childhood. Undoubtedly his imagination, foresight and positive approach were defining factors in much of the history of Rubelia. Michael always had a profound respect for Skipper's engineering skills as well as his uncanny ability to foresee the future. He went on to earn an engineering degree and was involved in the design and engineering of hydroelectric plants and refineries for the Flour Corporation. Later he was to start his own company doing analysis and monitoring of air quality and pollution for industrial and commercial buildings. Skipper's prediction of the flood confirmed for all time the aptness of Michael's phrase, "Skipper's always right, you know."

DWAYNE HUNN. Dwayne had come to Glendora after a stint in the Peace Corps assisting the poor in the slums of India. He was attending Claremont University to get his Masters Degree. Looking for a place to rent, he was steered to the Pharm by a local realtor who was aware of Michael's various rentals. Finding Michael in dirty overalls and floppy hat, he inquired about the possibility.

"Who said I had a place for rent," Michael wanted to know, and upon hearing of the referral, said, "Well, I might have a place. I don't know if the guy is going to choose his girlfriend or the Tree House." Apparently she had given the boyfriend an ultimatum, not being enchanted by the living conditions nestled in the embrace of the oak tree.

"Want to take a look at it?" he asked Dwayne, who agreed, being somewhat intrigued. Unable to climb the rotting stairs to the upper level dwelling, Michael then offered him a ladder to climb and look in the window. It was in as bad condition as the stairs, and when Dwayne started to climb the rickety device, Michael took off his hat and covered his face, fully expecting a disaster.

Dwayne said he would take the Tree House if the boyfriend made his choice from the heart. Michael then took Dwayne into the Big Kitchen for a pot of tea and some conversation about life in general and the possibilities of his future tenancy. The meeting lasted over an hour and Dwayne said that Michael admitted later that he had not really been taken with him because of his liberal leanings. He did, however, rent to Dwayne when the boyfriend and his lady left because he was a man of his word, and since Dwayne had climbed the ladder, he didn't really think he could refuse.

Dwayne remained on the Pharm for five years, joining in all of the major projects and liberation forays occurring during that period. He began teaching at a local high school after completing graduate school, and he and his students were crucial in the effort to save the Pharm and its neighbors during the 1969 flood and mudslide. He also authored a series of delightful articles for the *Glendoran* magazine entitled, "Every Town Needs a Castle," providing insightful and humorous glimpses into the lives of some of the builders.

Dwayne ultimately earned a Doctorate Degree and presently lives in Mill Valley, California, teaching Government and Management Studies at the University of San Francisco and Dominican College. He also exceeded the expectations of all his mentors in the early years at the Castle. While acknowledging that he didn't know a pipe wrench from a pair of pliers, he was always a most willing student and was attracted to the need for resourcefulness at the Castle. And the Pharm hands always teased him in those first years. "Dwayne, do you know why we pick on you so much?" Michael asked him one time. "Because if you pick on someone hard enough, they get better."

Well, he got so much better that his home now boasts a fully equipped shop in the garage, leaving no room for a car, but allowing him to exercise the mechanical skills acquired at the Castle. His writings are obvious witness to the life skills developed in both India and Glendora.

BILL GRAHAM. Bill had been transferred by the U. S. Forest Service to the Glendora area, as the Deputy Forest Supervisor of the Angeles National Forest, which included the San Gabriel Mountains. Living down the street from the Pharm, it wasn't long before he was introduced to Michael. Sharing many similar passions, such as the need for ongoing projects demanding both creativity and skill, the devotion to hoaxing, and the camaraderie which was inherent in Castle life, he quickly became one of Michael's many contributors. Bill left Glendora in a few years to become the Assistant Regional Forester for the California Region in San Francisco. After his retirement, Bill undertook the development and management of the Petaluma Municipal Airport, which soon became the fastest growing airport in California, and a model for the compatible integration of an airport into its community.

MICHAEL KEITH. Known as the "Lord High Chancellor," was eight years younger than Michael and a neighbor on Leadora Avenue. He started coming to the Pharm as a young boy even though his parents tried to discourage the practice. His father thought the atmosphere there was a bad influence, but Keith persisted. He was the primary "gofer" in the early years and everyone called him "Kiddo", but he was willing to do anything for the cause. He also had a fine-honed sense of hoaxing which would rival that of any Pharm hand.

On one occasion Dorothy had brought clients to the Tin Palace for tea before looking for a home to purchase. Her son was at sea with Boggs at the time and she had so informed her clients. Michael Keith happened to be in the wine cellar at the moment and Dorothy, seeing the open elevator shaft, called down, "Michael, are you down there?"

"Let me out of here!" Keith called back in a distressed voice. "I haven't had any food for a week! I don't have any water! Let me out of this place."

Dorothy, used to such pranks, walked on without paying attention. But the clients naturally thought "Michael" was her son who was supposedly at sea. This occurred just after Edith Friesner had told Dorothy, in front of the clients, she was going to dye Dorchen's dog blue if they didn't get rid of it, because the white hair made cleaning the blue carpet impossible.

This was the last straw for the clients, who bolted out the Palace door without explanation and disappeared. They had left their car at Dorothy's office and it remained there for three days. Dorothy was quite surprised, thinking the people would understand that the voice coming from the basement was just joking. Dorothy was more than adept and could hold her own with any of the Pharm hands when it came to hoaxing. Keith went into education and is presently a high school teacher in the State of Washington.

TED SHEPHERD. One of the most humorous of all the Castle residents, as we have seen from his letter. He never did much work, but he definitely was helpful in pointing out rocks and bottles for the other workers to gather. He brought morale to a new high, when he announced that there would be no telephone bills sent to the Pharm for as long as he lived there. Dorothy had been getting concerned because Ted was making calls all over the country on her phone. Somewhat skeptical, she called the Telephone Company and was advised that there was a notation on her account that it not be billed. It turned out that Ted's father was an Executive with American Telephone and Telegraph.

Ted also saw to it that no book had ever been written previously about Michael and the Castle. A man had begun work on the project many years ago and he had contacted Ted for a perspective on the whole story. Ted had responded to the prospective author, expressing doubt about the project, "because Michael Rubel is not really Michael Rubel. He is an imposter. The real Michael Rubel was killed in Algeria during the French Algerian War. The man who came back to Glendora is an imposter."

The writer was quite dismayed but, at Ted's suggestion, contacted Chris Rubel, Michael's brother, to determine if the imposter story were true. Ted had sent a blind copy of the letter to Chris. When the budding author approached Chris, the information he received was predictable.

"Well, he looked a lot like Michael when he returned from Algeria, but he didn't really seem to know anybody here. We were suspicious." The writer decided he should confront Michael with the newfound information. Michael had heard nothing about the

145

deception, but saw an opportunity when asked if he were really Michael Rubel.

"I've got a Driver's License and Passport that say I'm Michael Rubel."

"I know," the poor misled man replied, "but are you an imposter?"

"I'd be a fool to admit anything like that," Michael answered, looking around the Castle grounds, "I could lose all of this if I did."

As a last resort, the man approached Dorothy who also knew nothing of Ted's letter. She was asked if her son were an imposter.

"Well, he probably is," she answered, throwing her arms up, "But I don't know what I can do about it."

The discouraged writer abandoned the project, explaining that he didn't know whom to believe anymore, and that he would not want to be responsible for authoring something which might not be true.

Ted unquestionably left his mark wherever he went. He subsequently went to work for the Federal Government in Washington, D.C. and retired a few years ago as a Senior Auditor with the General Accounting Office. But he is still a Pharm hand at heart.

RON RIEGEL. Ron lived at the Castle for many years, sometimes using his truck to haul necessary building materials for the work crews, but more often a great motivator. When Michael would be relaxing, Ron would accuse him of malingering and say something like, "You'll never get that damned castle built if you don't get out of that hammock." Ron is a talented teacher, specializing in drafting, technical drawing and architecture. He still does stained glass work and antique restoration at the Castle. Ron is also an accomplished poet and wrote the following verse entitled *Michael's Dream*:

"In days of boyhood, reverie past,

Michael dreamed a lifelong task,

'Twas only daydreamed thoughts of child,

But in his mind this vision filed.

Now that Michael is a man,

His dream is more than just a plan,

Although this man-sized dream came true

He still does dream the dreams boys do."

JACK STIMSON. Jack donated the antique printing equipment to the Castle. This hand-set press is a 1912 model which was used in Pismo Beach in the 1930's. He had originally planned to go into the printing business, but military service redirected his talents and he is now a specialist in movie projection matters. Scott Rubel will still use the printing press for special projects, such as antique wedding invitations, but it is a laborious endeavor because of the time required to set the type.

PAUL FRITZ. Paul lived next door to the Rubels and would always come over and help, particularly by mixing concrete. Paul is one of the few Pharm hands that Michael has lost contact with and has been unable to locate.

JOHN McHANN. John and Michael grew up together and he was a constant contributor to the entire project. Like Skipper, John was also going to Engineering School at Cal Poly and had creative solutions for many of the complex problems facing the Castle builders for most of the construction years. John worked as an engineer for McDonald Douglas and Boeing Aircraft. He is now a specialist on surveillance cameras for satellites and high-altitude aircraft.

EDITH FRIESNER. Certainly the most enigmatic of all the Castle forces, Mrs. Friesner not only cleaned the Tin Palace and the Castle, but published her own handwritten newspaper, *The Shriek*, as Ted Shepherd has reported. Dwayne Hunn relates that the paper was more likely than not to contain supposedly secret personal items such as, "Dwayne had a date Saturday night, but the girl is not likely to go out with him again." Perhaps the key to the whole mystery is that Edith, who cleaned for many of the most influential people in town, was known as the Pharm Witch. In order to alleviate the burden of cleaning these spacious premises, she enacted a law that is still in effect at the Castle, "All ye who enter here, remove ye shoes and wear clean socks lest a curse be hung upon you." Even The Archbishop of Canterbury was required to observe the proclamation.

There is some evidence to validate Mrs. Friesner's occult powers. On one occasion Michael's phone rang and he was startled to hear Edith inform him that Bill Graham had gone into the Tin Palace with his shoes on, and that a two-hour curse was being placed upon him. Michael had no idea how she was aware that Bill was in the large building because she was not at the Pharm at all. When Michael investigated, he found Graham doing some work, and having forgotten to remove his shoes. They laughed off the threat, but when Bill tried to start his truck to leave, it gave no sign of life. Neither of them could find anything wrong, so Michael advised Bill to just relax, have a cup of tea and wait for two hours to elapse. Sure enough, the engine started without difficulty when the time was up. Michael still has no explanation for the occurrence, certain that no one tampered with the truck.

Michael came to love Edith Friesner dearly, and she has always been accorded a place of honor at the Castle through the observance of her proclamation. Michael's loving embrace of the people in his world is something which cannot be adequately described. Suffice it to say that the computer database of the friends he remains in contact with numbers over twelve hundred.

KAIA POORBAUGH. Kaia was a neighbor during most of the building years and assumed the role of historian for the Castle project. She has chronicled virtually all of the progress with a series of forty-two large picture albums depicting the complexity of the work. Kaia was born in Estonia and resided there as a child during World War II when the Country was first overrun by the German army moving into Russia, and then ravaged a second time when the Russian army reversed the flow of battle. She vividly recalls hiding in trenches as each country's air force alternately bombed her home, killing two of her eight siblings. Starvation was a constant threat and the family finally escaped from the Germans near the end of the War.

Kaia is a graduate of Penn State University and presently does special research work in the library at Claremont College, being capable of researching sources all over the world for students who require such assistance. Kaia can research materials in seven languages: Russian, Estonian, Finnish, French, German, Spanish and English. The story of Michael and Kaia's wedding is most poignant and will be saved for the last chapter.

JOHN McCAFFERTY. Michael and John became friendly in the 1960's and he was often a big help for undertakings requiring his heavy equipment. John would never charge Michael and was quite instrumental in saving Rubelia at the time of the flood. The wall Michael had built was breached and the mud was threatening to completely inundate the entire Pharm. Michael called John and told him he had no money but that help was needed immediately. John was working on another project, but told Michael he would be there in five minutes. He worked for endless hours and probably managed to avert a complete disaster by redirecting the flow of the mud with his bulldozer.

John also donated the Santa Fe caboose to the Pharm, which is probably the most popular attraction for the thousands of school kids who visit the Castle each year. This equipment is in excellent condition and is fully furnished down to the last detail. Air brake maintenance books, shipping logs, safety regulations and route information still inhabit the caboose as they did in operating years. The furnishings include bunks, brakeman's working table, kitchen, overhead observation seats, bathroom, and bathtub. The caboose, as we now see it, might have just completed a cross-country trip as home to the trainmen. John and Michael were refused a permit to move the caboose on the city streets to the Pharm from San Dimas, so they utilized Castle protocol and did it in the middle of the night, finally lifting it over the wall and setting it on the tracks inside with a crane.

      The Pharm hands constitute a most unique array of talent. When examined individually, the group would appear more appropriately as the board of directors of a major corporation, rather than the dedicated pursuers of the impossible dream. Perhaps the idea of success needs re-evaluation. Perhaps an essential element of that elusive goal is found in the deepest recesses of a person's character where there is a realization that success is both intensely individual and spiritual, and finds no parallel on a material level. If so, their "success" in life may well have originated in the passion that they shared with Michael Rubel.

ELEVEN

A Retrospective

"It is rich to live like a poor man."

"Truth is a very special thing – I only use
it on occasion."

Grandfather Deuel

The Castle was finally completed, and with it a unique era
came to a close. What was created and the manner in which it was
accomplished seems unparalleled in the post-World War II world.
There were no press releases announcing the completion, no
fanfare and certainly no civic celebration heralding the monument
on Live Oak Avenue in Glendora. For the Castle is only
emblematic of a time that men came together sharing a dream
because one man was convinced it would materialize.

It should not be assumed that the Castle was ignored by the
public or the media, for nothing could be further from the truth.
The list of visitors over the years ranges from President
Eisenhower to Henry Kissinger, from Rich Little, The World's
Slowest Rising Young Comedian, to Dustin Hoffman. It includes
Angie Dickinson, Prince Phillip of England, The Archbishop of
Canterbury and, more importantly, generations of school children
from almost everywhere, civic and senior's groups, the Sierra
Club, visitors from many countries, and thousands more who have
shared this fantasy. The magnificent pool table located at one end
of the Tin Palace is covered by a beautiful altar cloth, a gift from
the Archbishop of Canterbury, who was most impressed with this

unique work of art. The appeal of the Castle cuts across all ages and cultures; it fills a need for the child in us, for the part of us that resents increasing governmental intrusion in our lives, and especially for the spontaneity which many of us have submerged in our pursuit of "reasonable goals."

The television exposure for this phenomenon extends from the segment on the *Reasoner Reports* to the presentation done by Huell Howser on *California's Gold*. It would probably have also appeared on Barbara Walter's television program but for Michael's hesitancy when she approached him. Ms. Walters suggested that she might have an opportunity to do a segment since Harry Reasoner had been shown similar hospitality. Michael, not knowing who Barbara Walters was, and sensing another aggressive intrusion, admits to being terrified of her. He went into his backward, farm-boy mode when she made her request:

"Well, I don't really know. I'm not capable of making decisions. You'll have to ask my mother."

"Well, How did Harry Reasoner get to do his program?" Walters asked.

"I don't know," Michael said, "You'll have to ask my mother."

"I would like to talk to your mother then," Walters persisted, "and see if it can be arranged."

Michael gave her directions to Dorothy's office and quickly got on the phone as soon as she departed. Dorothy, of course, knew who Barbara Walters was and generously explained that the

Reasoner filming had created too much of a disturbance in the residential neighborhood and it simply could not be allowed again.

The Castle completion did not go unobserved. But it was reserved for all of the Pharm hands and their families, as well as the neighbors who had supported the project in so many ways. The invitation read:

> You are invited to the Rubel Castle May 4, 1986
> At Four in the Afternoon – Sunday. You will not be permitted to leave the castle until 9:30 that same evening.
> Black Tie optional – Long Dresses Requested.
> R.S.V.P. by April 20, 1986
> Present this invitation at the gate upon arrival.

Over one hundred fifty guests attended the gala and almost all were in formal dress. The Castle courtyard was the scene of an endless supply of champagne and hors d'oeuvres, while the guests congratulated themselves and Michael for the miracle they had wrought. The bottles of bubbly were appropriately buried in mountains of ice in the mining cars and the blacksmith's iron pots that grace the courtyard. It could not have been a more perfect ending for the years of sweat, toil, harassment, and perseverance.

But after an hour or so of socializing, Michael began to express concern that the caterers had not shown up. Half an hour later Michael again voiced his distress, saying that he didn't know what he would do since it appeared that they were not coming at all.

"Michael, you have this many people and you don't have any food?" voiced a very upset Louise Lawton, who had always, since Michael's childhood, been critical of his lack of proper decorum. (After all, this was the same Michael who, as a boy, with Skipper Landon, had decided to slide down the three-story laundry chute in the Lawton home during a formal dinner party. Since the landing area in the basement was unforgiving, they had piled the guests' fur coats and outerwear in a pile at the outlet to soften the landing. Unfortunately the pile included a very expensive Homburg belonging to one of the guests, and it was destroyed. Michael had served a term cutting the Lawton's lawn for this indiscretion.)

"I just don't know what I can do," Michael bemoaned, distressed at the non-appearance of the caterers, but then an idea came to him.

"I'll call some friends and have them bring over some school buses," Michael declared, "and they will take us all to a restaurant."

Four buses arrived in due time and Michael herded all of the guests in their fancy clothing into vehicles which were designed for children. Louise was mortified that she should be subjected to such treatment. Michael directed the drivers to take them all to a small diner in town which could not possibly handle a crowd of this size. When they debarked from the buses, Michael dismissed them and they drove off. Michael then peered in the front window of the diner which, by now, everyone could see was closed.

"Well, I guess we'll just have to walk back to the Castle," was Michael's reply to Louise, who was almost livid at this point. Picture the scene: one hundred fifty persons dressed in black tie and formal wear wandering around the sidewalks of Glendora on a

Sunday afternoon, looking for a place to eat. It was becoming a distinctly Rubelian operation.

Just then the four buses drove around the corner at the end of the block and were hailed in time. They all boarded and Michael directed the drivers to take the group to a McDonald's.

"I've never eaten in one of those places in my life," Louise complained.

"Well it's really good, Louise," Michael tried reassuring her.

But the manager of the fast food restaurant came out and quickly informed them that they could not possibly handle a crowd of that size. So they all re-boarded the buses once again. At this juncture, there were those among the guests who began to sense the Rubel Straight Face factor coming into play. But not Louise.

"Michael, you're just hopeless," was all she could say, satisfied that Michael would never understand the particulars of entertaining.

The bus drivers were then told to proceed to a fine restaurant in nearby Cucamonga, *The Sycamore Inn*. "You just can't come to a good restaurant like this without a reservation," Louise berated Michael, but when they entered a large dining room reserved for the occasion, decorated with flowers and candles, it became obvious to all but one of the guests that the whole scenario had just been another Rubel hoax. The wonderful prime rib dinner was accompanied by fine wines, and the entire entourage had a true celebration fit for a King and his Court.

One last surprise remained for Louise. By prearrangement, one of the bus drivers told the party that they had been arrested for stealing the school buses and were being taken to jail. Predictably, she was quite unhappy when Michael said that they would all probably have to walk home because the buses were being impounded. But Louise finally understood that there are no limits to Michael's sense of humor and she was able to join in the celebration marking the memorable occasion.

The City of Glendora, which had originally been Michael's dedicated antagonist, finally joined the ranks of Rubelians after the flood. And in due time formal recognition came in the form of a Proclamation which was adopted unanimously by the City Council. This was an event that took Michael completely by surprise. Nick Moffitt had arranged to take Michael out to dinner, but he arrived in a limousine that was escorted by a large contingent of Glendora Police cars and motorcycles.

Nick placed a crown on Michael's head that had been fashioned by Warren Asa, the Castle Blacksmith, and Kaia fitted a regal cape over his shoulders for the ride to City Hall. When Michael asked Nick the purpose of the crown, he admitted that it was, "so they can see you're a goofball." This concession to the Rubelian sense of irreverence being completed, they entered the Council Chambers packed with the many of the citizens of Glendora. The session was opened by the Mayor after the Pledge of Allegiance and the National Anthem. The following Proclamation was read by the Mayor to the assemblage:

157

PROCLAMATION

WHEREAS Michael Clarke Rubel was born April 16, 1940, the son of Henry Scott Rubel and Dorothy Deuel Rubel, and;

WHEREAS As a citizen of Glendora, his kindness, generosity and public spirit are a Legend in Glendora, and;

WHEREAS Mike Rubel has created from an original citrus packing house and its surrounding properties a unique world known as Rubel Farms, and;

WHEREAS Rubel Farms stands in value to the community as a preserve of antiques, artifacts, memorabilia, and remembrances of yesterday, and;

WHEREAS Mike Rubel has served as a gracious host to thousands of visitors to Rubel Farms, including friends, neighbors, service clubs, educational organizations, newspapers, television, philanthropic groups and seekers of the uncommon, and;

WHEREAS he has shown unselfish devotion to Glendora and its residents through his work at Rubel Farms;

NOW THEREFORE, I, Guy A. Williams Jr., Mayor of the City of Glendora, do hereby recognize with appreciation Mike Rubel's outstanding service and contributions to the betterment of Glendora;

IN WITNESS WHEREOF, I have hereunto set my hand and caused the Seal of the City of Glendora to be affixed this 12th Day of April, 1983.

/s/ Guy A. Williams, Jr.

Michael's life changed dramatically in a few ways once the Castle was completed, and remained the same in most others. He is still the ever-optimistic, cheerful, humorous and caring person who presided over this unusual period in the history of Glendora. He is still conscious of the power that guides all of us, and trusts in that power to provide for our every need. He still values friendship over wealth, possessions and power, but holds sacred the power of freedom which we all possess in abundance. He once became so concerned with the heritage of freedom that he decided to run for the Glendora City Council. This was while the Castle was still under construction.

Michael never quite had the guile that now seems to be necessary in politics. Nick Moffitt had been his campaign manager, and realized part way through the campaign that his election might bring about changes that none of his supporters thought desirable. About two weeks before the election Michael noticed a 4' x 8' sign posted in town that read in bold blue letters on a white background: "What the Hell, Vote for Rubel, One man can't ruin everything."

"How can you do something like that?" Michael asked Nick.

"We decided that we didn't want you on the City Council," Nick explained reasonably, "because you'll have to become too mature and respectable."

At a public forum for the candidates held by the League of Women Voters, Nick had put up a sign at the entrance that read, "Rubel believes women shouldn't be allowed to vote." Michael was unaware of the sign and when asked by one of the questioners whether he believed women should not be allowed a vote, he responded, humorously, "Well, of course." That gaffe and the fact that he stated to the assemblage that he had no qualifications for the position, assured a landslide defeat. In retrospect, he realizes that election would have made it almost impossible for him to have completed the unique work to which he had dedicated his life.

One of the major changes in Michael's life after the Castle was the disability caused by the back surgery he had undergone. He suffered debilitating pain for four years after the surgery and was dependent on many of the Pharm hands for the completion of the construction. The back surgery had devastating results and his neck became immobilized, a condition which became permanent.

Michael was obliged to discontinue driving the school bus, much to his disappointment. He loved the kids and had developed a profound respect for the younger generations through his years of association with them. This is one of the reasons that tours for kids' groups are a major priority at the Castle. The disability has also prevented him from any driving activity since the operation, and it is very difficult to take care of even routine maintenance items at the Pharm. The disability, however, has been incapable of impairing his cheerfulness, positive outlook and profound appreciation for the gifts he has been blessed with.

The gift Michael has been most blessed with is Kaia. After so many years as a neighbor and Pharm hand, her life had changed and she became a single mother. Michael was rather reticent to ask her out, and when he did, she was even more reluctant. It took some persuasion, but she finally consented to go out to dinner with him. Castle building had relegated dating to one of Michael's more undeveloped talents, and probably could be the subject of another story. Suffice it to say that they developed a nice relationship, but one which Kaia was unwilling to have culminate in marriage. "Why should we get married when we have such a good relationship," she would answer when Michael broached the subject, "and marriage might ruin it?" This was the status quo until 1996. Here we should pause to let Michael tell the story:

OUR WEDDING

Michael and Kaia

Does everyone get asked about their marriage as often as we do? There is probably a good reason that we get quizzed.

Eight years ago I asked Kaia to marry me. She reasoned that our relationship was so perfect that it would be best to leave our lives as is. There were good reasons for this decision, but reason seldom makes a man happy when making this important partnership.

We decided to take a trip around the world. Many of you may remember getting our post cards. We had a wonderful trip. When we arrived in Bad

Homburg v.d.H., where I had attended school in 1958, I looked up a friend Helmut Barth and asked him if he would meet us in Helsingor, Denmark and play the organ for a possible wedding: mine. He was delighted. His reputation is such that he has carte blanche with many cathedrals in Europe to play their organs. I contacted Walter Rosenthal, a good friend living in Denmark, and asked him (we worked together on the S.S. Barachias in the 1960's) if he would meet us at Helsingor Domkirke (built between 1200 and 1500). I explained my hope that in this setting Kaia would marry me. I asked him to ask some of our mutual friends to come on the 21st of May. He was delighted with the plan.

Kaia asked me about my excited attitude. She is perceptive. We took a tower room near the Church and Helmut Barth took a room next to ours. Kaia was incredulous that Helmut roomed next to us but let it go as just another example of a "small world" moment. Eighteen people met us at the Church, where, Helmut made arrangements to play the organ which he had participated in rebuilding in 1969.

We gathered and he played the Toccata and Fugue in D Minor by J.S. Bach which was truly incredible. He pulled out all the stops and it was magnificent. I had asked Walter to have our friends file by Kaia and ask her to please marry Michael. By the fourth man she began to cry. Nothing is more heart wrenching than to see Kaia crying. Everyone was mortified. I asked her to marry me. She said yes

with tears running down her cheeks. We all had
tears. It was truly an emotional event with Helmut
playing softly the wedding march.

The minister, who was a friend of one of my
shipmates, married us informally. When Kaia said,
"Yes, I will," the minister made everyone smile by
inserting, "Thank the Lord."

When we exited the Church, there were people
waiting to get in. I later found out that there had
been a radio announcement that Helmut Barth
would play. He was able to join our party later that
evening.

It was explained to me that I was put to bed with a
smile on my face. WHAT A DAY!

Any retrospective should necessarily look toward the future
of the Castle, for its rich legacy and singular design must be
preserved for future generations. The artistic endeavor responsible
for its creation contains a history that is both educational and
inspirational. There is nothing comparable in the United States,
and the genius and tenacity of its creators must eventually be
recognized through its designation as a monument of historical
significance. Such recognition may not come easily for there are
barriers to be overcome.

The conflict between the City and Michael did not
disappear with the dismissal of the criminal charges against him.
The official harassment continued until an agreement was finally

reached and reduced to a written contract. It essentially provides for three major conditions:

1. That the Castle would never be used for commercial purposes.

2. That nothing would be built high enough to fall on a neighboring property. The city originally wanted this condition to read, "on a public right of way," but Michael refused to agree to this condition since the towers all rise far above the public streets. The City finally asked Michael how he wanted it to read, and this is how the existing language was adopted.

3. That anything built without a permit would automatically be condemned. The City Fathers asked Michael if he realized the implications of this provision. He, of course, understood that it meant that the Pharm could never be sold.

The Agreement was reached because Michael believes that the City Government was incapable of dealing with someone who is not motivated by profit or salability, with someone who did not mind if he went to jail for defending his inalienable rights, and most certainly with someone who had the steadfast support of much of the community. There had been a promise of a recall election for the entire City Council if Michael were sent to jail. What a marvelous example of pure democracy in action!

These are the barriers confronting the preservation of the Castle. In the short term, Michael will obviously live there for the rest of his life, for it is his home and his joy. And he will continue to make it available to the many groups who want to tour the edifice and learn of its history. Richard Macy, Warren Asa, Warren Bowen and Jim Riley are the docents who so willingly donate their time and talents to this effort, and they are the modern day Pharm hands to whom Michael is so indebted, for the ongoing tours are far too tiring a task for one person to undertake. They also arrange the tours so that they are not intrusive to the beautiful neighborhood surrounding the Castle.

Nor has Michael ignored the long term. He has provided in his Will that the Castle be left to the Glendora Historical Society, confident that under its stewardship the beauty of this creation will endure and be available to those who have yet to experience its charms. The Society already maintains a beautiful museum in the old City Hall and Jail, and recognizes the wonderful heritage that must be preserved for the community. The commercial restriction on the property should not be a hindrance to the Society, which could certainly create a class of membership that would entitle members to visit the Castle on planned tours similar to those now being conducted. For Michael has never wanted to be less than a good neighbor, and would like that relationship preserved in the future.

Sitting in his overstuffed chair on the porch of the Castle, smoking his pipe and watching the scores of hummingbirds darting around the several feeders, and observing the occasional hawk flying over looking longingly for baby geese or chickens, Michael is a man who is truly happy. He has his Castle and his Queen, and a never-ending stream of friends. He has memories that would nourish anyone for several lifetimes and he still maintains the spontaneity and the faith which propelled him through his youth and adulthood. Sitting there with his ever-present smile, he reflected:

"I'm just so thankful and grateful. Just to be able to sit here and enjoy everything, and to have someone like Kaia to share it with. I'm so blessed and I just don't understand why. We've traveled over the world to many beautiful places, but we can't imagine anything as beautiful as our home in the Castle in beautiful Glendora. I don't think I'm bright enough to know what I should have done. There were things I've done that were not very smart, but they always worked out. There must be a higher power that always keeps things opening up for me. I just always expect things to work out. And they do."

Michael's reflections, and his life, hold a message for those who would dare to dream. Remember, that once a castle was built with only a dream, and the belief that the means to accomplish it would always be there. That same potential is within each of us if we will only believe unquestionably in the power that Michael knows exists. That is his legacy to Rubelians everywhere.

THE END